Church and State

Church and State

The English Experience

The Prideaux Lectures for 1990

Adrian Hastings

University of Exeter Press

First published in 1991 by
University of Exeter Press
Reed Hall, Streatham Drive
Exeter EX4 4QR
UK

www.exeterpress.co.uk

© Adrian Hastings 1991

A catalogue record for this book is available from the British Library.

ISBN 9780859893688

For
Susan and Patrick

Contents

Preface	ix
1 Patterns of Dualism	1
2 The Triumph and Decline of Justinianism	16
3 A Tradition of Dissent	33
4 What Matters To Us Now	51
Epilogue	67
Further Reading	77
Index	81

Preface

I am very grateful to the Trustees of the Bishop John Prideaux Lecture Fund for the invitation to give the 1990 Prideaux Lectures in the University of Exeter. The Vice-Chancellor, the Bishop and Dean of Exeter and David Catchpole, the Professor of Theological Studies, all made of it no mere formal invitation but a continuously warm welcome and an exceptionally happy experience. It gave me the opportunity to present in brief a carefully pondered personal view, theological and historical, of what has been one of the central realities of both Christian and national life.

The four lectures are presented here essentially as they were delivered last February and March. The Epilogue, however, is an addition written this September.

I am grateful as ever to Ingrid Lawrie, my secretary, not only for typing the lectures but for the constant support which made it more possible to write them. Yet being my secretary is only a small part of her duties as writing lectures is only a small part of mine.

Adrian Hastings
Leeds, 25 September 1990

Chapter One

Patterns of Dualism

PASSUS SUB PONTIO PILATO. Our starting point is a criminal's execution. We can be sure of the cross. We can be sure that Jesus of Nazareth's natural life ended in a condition of total powerlessness, condemned and executed by the state, the civil power of the Roman Empire supported by Jewish authority. We can be reasonably sure too, despite the arguments of Brandon to the contrary, that Jesus's execution did not reflect any commitment by Jesus to political action of a revolutionary sort. Jesus was neither allied to the state nor an enemy of the state, from which he sought nothing. He was not a sadducee but he was not a zealot either. If he has to be categorised—but essentially his greatest claim to a unique authority may lie in his radical inability to be categorised—it would be as some sort of radical pharisee, a prophetic teacher of religious and moral truth, proclaiming the nearness and farness of a kingdom of God which was both infinitely more and infinitely less than the kingdom of Caesar.

Two other things of which we can also be sure need to be included within our starting point. First, if Jesus's 'kingdom' and concerns were, in a straightforward way, neither for nor against 'the state', they nevertheless included it and its affairs as part of a world, part of its furniture one might say, within which the Kingdom was to be realised. 'Render to Caesar the things that are Caesar's and to God the things that are God's' remains one of the most difficult and enigmatic of sayings to interpret, but its sense does seem to include the recognition that there are some things, if perhaps deeply unimportant things, which do properly belong to Caesar. Political obligation is affirmed—as it is later by Paul in Romans—as one of the still valid requirements of the present age, but it is radically distinguished from religious obligation, as required by the eschatological Kingdom of God. There is in this saying, just as there is in the Crucifixion, a dualism which will remain for ever integral to the central Christian tradition. In practical terms to decide what is of Caesar, what of God, was and is the problem. Any short saying is bound to seem simplistic. What this saying does is to make some room in God's world for obligation to a ruler, even an unbelieving ruler. Isaiah had already done the same for Cyrus, Jeremiah for Nebuchadnezzar. It does not withdraw the things of Caesar from God's world, and it would be much misused if one were to infer a sharp division of the things of this world into two separate almost equal realms. There can exist secondary obligations, it says, which are not specifically religious but still are valid. But, above all, do not confuse things by giving to Caesar any more than his due.

If Jesus, as earlier prophets, could admit a dualism of immediate authority, he could not—any more than they—admit that matters of justice and injustice, of the use of wealth and power to discriminate against and ill-use the poor and the weak could possibly be excluded from the concern of religion. The world of work and trade, marriage and tax-gathering, is the world of God. Jesus is asking neither for a withdrawal from this world nor for its bureaucratic religious control. There is no sign that he condemned the use of money, or marriage, or of political power, of wine or work or play. There is no sign that he wanted his followers to withdraw from any of these things or that, for the most part, they thought they should withdraw—radically temporary as the use of all things of this world must be seen to be. Yet his teaching affected, and was bound to affect, the use of all such things. He had himself been so marginal to all of them: unmarried, homeless, workless, at the end the almost naked criminal outcast, the man whom Jew and Gentile could agree to condemn.

The immediately marginal is declared to be in reality central while the immediately central is declared essentially only provisional. It is natural enough that in consequence his followers should at times sit lightly to the claims of marriage, work, or government. The gap between Jesus and everything else does not condemn everything else, but it does engender an on-going ambiguity touching the relationship between his religion and the things of this world, an ambiguity symbolised most strikingly in insistence at once upon the sacrament of marriage and the value of celibacy. It is the interaction of the two which constitutes the enigmatic wholeness of the Christian understanding of the physical and the sexual. The practice of monasticism, with its commitment to a radical withdrawal from the normalities of human life—marriage and the possession of property—has often been a possibly simplistic attempt to recreate an idealised early church life, Jesus's life itself. If overplayed, this line of Christian commitment inevitably depreciates marriage and the normalities of the created, secular world. If underplayed, the mysterious freedom engendered by the figure of Jesus in regard to all the norms of this world is likely to be lost. The memory of Jesus has over the centuries engendered a mysterious interplay between the freedom of marginality and the constraining responsibilities of identification with the secular, whether marital or political. Essentially there is here from the start a strategy of dualism: an assertion of otherness—of the necessity for the proclamation of a new dimension—but without withdrawal or condemnation. It is this ability to be in, but not wholly of, which fundamentally creates in the political field the church/state dilemma. It is, then, a dilemma derived from the most fundamental roots of Christianity: a radical inability to be either politicised or apolitical while remaining true to itself. It has to acknowledge the state, it has to keep a certain distance from the state, it has to be concerned in its own way with what the state is concerned with. To do all that at one and the same time is never easy.

We may see the point of all this better through making a comparison with Islam. Muhammad was a political as well as a religious leader and he established a community which was as political as it was religious, based upon a very precise law and including institutions of violence, both penal and military. There were no rules to define the structure of government, but a political society has to have government and Muhammad as its ruler had defined the form of government to a considerable extent by his own behaviour. He was succeeded by the Caliphs and, as Islam has no priests, there was no other succession (except for that of physical descent from one of his considerable number of wives: here again Muhammad was as central to sexual activity as Jesus was marginal to it). The Islamic State, ruled for centuries by the Caliphs, is the normative pattern for Islam and Muslims living outside the Islamic State remain in principle abnormal. In adhering to the central and original idea of Islam they can only hope and work to rectify this abnormality, in the Sudan, Nigeria or Britain, by establishing an Islamic State and the observance of the Sharia. Moreover, 'an' Islamic State is itself misleading. The original conception of Islam was of a single Islamic State—there could be no point in there being more than one, for the state is not defined by language, race or location, but by adherence to Islam. And for centuries there was but one. The Islamic State necessarily and naturally wiped away existing frontiers to establish a new unity at once religious and political.

The political and the violent are, then, from the time of Muhammad integral elements in both the theory and the practice of Islam. From the time of Jesus and for centuries afterwards they were alien elements in both the theory and practice of Christianity. The contrast in this regard between the two great world religions deriving from the Middle East out of hebraic source material is profound and the actual similarity in various periods in their use of the political must not be allowed to obscure the root principled difference between them: Islam has an ideal political model written into its foundation charter, Christianity has none. Today when in many parts of the world the interaction of politics and religion is an issue of vital importance functioning within at least three very different thought contexts—the Christian, the Islamic and the secularist—it is vital to be able to disengage the starting points of all three. A lazy inability to distinguish the Christian from the Islamic within the fuzzy construct of 'the religious' can be helpful to no-one. This brief consideration of the Islamic starting point is intended simply to sharpen by contrast our sense of the far less determinate character of the Christian one. To this may be added reference to the undeniable gap in experience between Jesus and the church such as does not exist between Muhammad and the Umma: Jesus's apparent failure to say anything much about the church, to provide any sort of detailed law, or to suggest how the problems with which the church was likely to be faced could be resolved, all this gave a great freedom to the church to alter and develop in subsequent ages without a sense of infidelity to its foundation charter.

This freedom offers both strength and weakness: the ability to grow with and respond to the cultures of the world, in many ages and places, upon the one hand, the absence of a simple, clear norm, upon the other. To be a Christian one has, in a sense, always to think theologically and contextually. Yet across that first gap separating Christ and the early church does stretch a common sense of otherness and relative unconcern in regard to the state: render to Caesar, indeed, but these remain secondary things, peripheral to Christian life. The Christian experience of the first centuries was to remain the emperor's good servant, but God's first: to obey the state (Romans 13 and I Peter 2) but quite often to suffer from it, 'dragged before princes and kings' (Matthew 10 and Revelation 13); to seek for a quiet life but to be ready for martyrdom; to take absolutely for granted a chasm dividing the institutions of the church—baptism and eucharist, presbyters and bishops—from the institutions of the state— armies and taxes, governors and emperors (a chasm which can make no sense at all in the primary world of Islam, though of course in the secondary world of how things actually are within a minority condition, it makes perfect sense for many a devout Muslim. A crucial general question for modern society is how far Islam as such has the potential to develop a hermeneutic which can reinterpret the material of its original political model in a fairly definitive way. Pragmatically it has in places done so, but the original model keeps reappearing as the ideal.

What altered the early Christian pattern of things decisively was the conversion of Constantine. The very decisiveness of that extra-ordinary development following upon the anguish of the Great Persecution has, however, reduced to an unjustified obscurity the previous state of things through much of the third century. It is worth turning our minds to that earlier period for a little while because it offers a model somewhat different from apostolic times and very different indeed from the Christian empire, yet it is a model which prefigures the modern predicament surprisingly well.

Everywhere Christians were a minority: in a few places (such as parts of lower Egypt and Cappadocia) a very large minority, in most places a relatively small one. They included all classes. The church was certainly not just a community of the very poor and it included some very senior imperial officials, if rather few. Its core was, almost everywhere, urban—artisans and shopkeepers, for the most part, with a smattering of intellectuals and upper-class ladies. It was not—at least by comparison with times to come—a highly institutionalised community and most of its leaders were unprofessionaly trained older married men. Bishops of the social class and intellectual calibre of Cyprian were most unusual. But it now possessed many hundreds of small church buildings, publicly recognisable as such, and even a perhaps cheekily placed cathedral opposite the imperial palace at Nicomedia. It had its convents, its cemeteries, its occasional local councils of bishops. It was, in modern terms, a denomination, neither withdrawn from society nor identical with it. The state recognised its bishops as moderately important people with whom, on occasion, it was necessary actually to do business. For the most part it was allowed to live in peace, despite a good deal of general suspicion, and its members occupied almost every position in society without any strident exhibition of Christian differentiation.

The Christian ideal for church-state relations in the third century seems a recognisably modern one: a free church in a neutral state: 'It is not in the nature of religion to compel religion' declared Tertullian. Nevertheless their growing number, their rather pacifist attitudes, and their official refusal to mix their religion with the cults of others, even the imperial cult itself, were naturally seen by many in power as dangerous. From time to time, in consequence, and more in some places than others, they were attacked, their buildings smashed, their bishops and other notables arrested and killed. It was not a church of martyrs and, by the third century, in times of persecution, the great majority of Christians compromised their faith. This general state of things—a free church tolerated by a benign state or persecuted by a more neurotic state—may well have seemed the clearly appropriate normative condition for church-state relations to Christians of the time, a condition which reflected well enough New Testament guidelines, such as they were, but mediated across the altered experience of a large, diversified yet not preponderant or politicised community.

It cannot, most of all in the west, have anticipated what was about to come. Constantine's conversion across Sun worship to Christianity is not plausibly to be interpreted as a predictable piece of political astuteness, leaping upon the bandwagon of a near dominant faith. He was fighting for control of the western empire and in the west Christians remained a quite small minority and not a particularly powerful one. The army, the bureaucracy, the senatorial class all remained and would long remain overwhelmingly pagan. Emperors had favoured various cults in the past and the ruling classes may not have felt at first particularly surprised or disturbed by this latest piece of personal imperial piety. Its institutionalised irreversability was not in the least obvious and, of course, a little too late Constantine's nephew Julian did try to reverse it. The Edict of Milan itself proclaimed no less but no more than what thoughtful third-century Christians had wanted: freedom of religion. 'To each man's judgement and will the right should be given to care for sacred things according to each man's own free choice'. That the consequences for Christians and non-Christians alike would soon prove so different was not immediately obvious. Conversion brought the emperor no very valuable support of a non-supernatural kind, at least in the west, and quite a few additional problems. The Christian church and its ever multiplying internal issues of belief and discipline appeared to need regulating quite as much as the imperial cult of the past. Constantine did not so much enter the church (he was only in fact baptised on his deathbed almost thirty years later) as graciously decide, in response to the personal protection God had given him, that the church should be brought within the inner circle of imperial favour and control. Very suddenly great basilicas were constructed, bishops received salaries, honorific titles and governmental duties, ecclesiastical schisms and doctrinal disagreements were dealt with by the emperor's summoning of councils and exiling of the refractory. Bishops could soon be appointed to command imperial armies and generals could be instructed to manage the church's affairs.

For those who, like the emperor himself, believed in the quite special divine providence behind all this, Constantine was hailed as 'Friend of God', 'universal bishop', thirteenth apostle, the man of providence called to fuse Christian belief and Roman order into a new unity. Such was the political philosophy of Eusebius of Caesarea, the leading bishop scholar of his age and author of the first really major account of Christian history ever to be written. It ends upon a note of quite extraordinary exultation about 'Constantine the most mighty victor . . . an Emperor most dear to God'. In comparison with such a figure, the successor of Augustus as much as of Christ, individual bishops appeared hopelessly insignificant. For the most part they did what they were told or kept quiet. Of few popes do we know less than of Sylvester, bishop of Rome for seventeen years during Constantine's reign. But the fusion of church and empire was only beginning in his reign. It was to be carried far further and more systematically by his son Constantius: 'What I decree let that be accounted a canon'. No ruler ever did more to impose doubtful doctrine upon the universal church and not only was Athanasius of Alexandria exiled for resisting imperial orthodoxy but so was Pope Liberius until he crumbled and capitulated. A quite revolutionary pattern of church-state relations was here rapidly emerging: a pattern of caesaropapism, at once pragmatic and ideological.

What must have seemed to Christians of that time an almost incredible numerical and institutional growth of the church connected with imperial support and all the new openings this allowed, the public liturgical centrality provided by the vast new imperially-funded basilicas, the worldly excitement of entry into the most influential corridors of establishment, wealth and power, all this produced a euphoria able temporarily to turn the heads of many a bishop less intelligent than Eusebius. Even Augustine could turn willingly enough to imperial authority to crush the obstinacy of local schismatic Christians. In the immediate vista there seemed so much to gain. Moreover there had been so little central authority in the church hitherto; bishops—even the bishops of Rome or Alexandria—had been such essentially small people that it is not surprising the church could seem quite bowled over by the embraces of autocracy served by a highly developed bureaucracy and standing army. It required the sheer bloody toughness of Athanasius not to surrender. Fortunately the continual meddling in high doctrine, the pressures exerted above all by Constantius, soon began to turn the new model rather sour. Nevertheless the peril was profound. The fundamental polity of the church was at stake: Constantine and Constantius were doing to Christianity what, three centuries later, Muhammad would do to the under-developed cults of Arabia. But, while the latter were unable to withstand the pressures of such politico-religious reorganisation to form a universalist monolithic unity, Christianity had rather more resources for resistance. It had a largely unformulated yet profoundly formative tradition received from Jesus and the apostolic church, and with this tradition the kind of order the emperors were trying to impose was not easily compatible.

In general, nevertheless, the church has lived with the politicisation resultant upon the Constantinian revolution from the fourth century until the twentieth in the way that the principal traditions of Christianity have taken for granted their right, whenever they can get it, to a position of special privilege and political power. They have seen establishment as normality, and have forgotten how late it came in Christian history. It is true that the west was less affected by the full thrust of Constantinianism than the east. Oddly enough, though the experiment was begun when Constantine was emperor of the west alone, its real development became centred upon his new capital of Constantinople. The heritage of Eusebius of Caesarea was Greek not Latin. Constantinople became the Greek capital of a Greek empire, suspected as much by Egypt as by Italy. Here were neither the traditional pagan loyalties of old Rome nor the claims of an apostolic see to counter the Constantinian myth and the embrace of imperial favour in all its bewitching magnificence. With Justinian an explicit and fully-formed Christian monism, a church-state led by a single prince both *Imperator* and *Pontifex Maximus*, became the abiding norm for Greek Christianity. While the developed order of the Byzantine church was not a totally state-controlled one (only very metaphorically could the emperor be *pontifex*; the existence even of a rather subservient patriarchate spoke of the survival of an underlying dualism), it was too far removed from the dualism of Christian origins to be very healthy. The sense of the necessity of a critical distancing between God and Caesar had been lost. This not only contributed to the parting of east and west, it produced within the east a bitter anti-Constantinople reaction in Egypt and Syria but it also engendered a far wider sense of the acceptability of erastianism continuing well into our own day. This has not served Greek and Russian Christianity too well. Absolutely every church tradition has been profoundly flawed (recognition of this should be the starting point of any sound historical ecclesiology) but the particular weakness of the post-Constantine and post-Justinian eastern tradition is that of an erastian monism—a weakness all the more dangerous because the very fidelity of the east in so much else to the central early balance of Christianity has often misled western Christians too from the time of Charlemagne on into seeing erastianism as acceptable in a way that it cannot, or should not, ever be. In any full-blooded erastianism the point of Pontius Pilate is forgotten, the Cross loses all political significance and becomes either a symbol only of personal sin and redemption or one of something terrible the Jews did, instead of signifying too a profound and mutually threatening distance within all societies between the authority of Jesus and the authority of Caesar.

The point we need to note here was that the pressures of imperial power in fact produced, at least in the west, less a replacement of dualism by monism in the field of church and state than the rejuvenation of dualism both institutionally and theologically. Only a strengthening of episcopal authority could at the time possibly save the church from a perpetuity of state control. The great development of the papacy in the period from Damasus through Leo to Gregory the Great may be seen far less as a take-over by the bishops of Rome of the traditional prestige of the imperial city than as a necessary defence of ecclesiastical freedom against political control. It was a defence fully in line, within the altered conditions of a Christianised empire, with the original dualism of church and state. *Duo sunt*, declared Pope Gelasius I in a much-quoted letter to the Emperor Anastasius I in 494: 'The world is chiefly governed by these two: the sacred authority of bishops and the royal power'. Neither authority is subordinate to the other because they are of quite different kinds. This papal assertion of dualism was backed by the most mature thinking of the greatest theologian of the Latin world. Augustine's construction of a world view based upon an on-going dialectical tension and contrast between two cities, heavenly and earthly, was profoundly different from a Eusebian view which saw the birth of Jesus in the time of Augustus as the self-evidently providential preparation for the merging of empire and church. Both Augustine's theology and the growth and teaching of the papacy stood firmly in the west for dualism and against monism, even if the post-Hildebrandine papacy with its ever wider claims for a divine 'plenitudo potestatis' from which the king received authority came later to undermine the critical distance from the state and the anti-monist position which the development of the papacy in an earlier era had stood for.

Our English church, for we can at last now actually begin to consider our chosen subject, began in the context of western post-Constantinianism. Church and society were loosely accepted as naturally coterminous and inter-concerned but their authorities remained sufficiently distinct. Indeed the circumstances in which the church took real root in England in the seventh century were almost a direct reversal of those of the fourth. Consider the towering figure of Theodore of Tarsus, Archbishop of Canterbury from 668 to 690. A Greek monk from Asia Minor in his late sixties, he seems an extraordinary choice for the Pope to nominate as archbishop for England and dispatch on a difficult journey to a far northern island. But what authority he came to have! He is described in the synodical letter produced by the Synod of Hatfield in 680 as 'Archbishop of the island of Britain and the city of Canterbury' and, even more charmingly, by a council at Rome the year before as

'Archbishop and philosopher of the Island of Britain'. This was a time when there was no political unity even within the south of England. Each of Theodore's suffragan bishops had to relate to a different tribal king, all of inevitably limited experience. Theodore's experience, learning, breadth of vision, sureness of touch, sheer pastoral authority must have overwhelmed. It was a pastoral and ecclesiastical authority, in no way a political one, yet Theodore successfully mediated between warring kings and he did much to establish the unique, if unformulatable, role of the Archbishops of Canterbury as a supra-political one, a role which has endured from his time to ours.

It is important to stress that this role precedes that of the monarchy. A generation after Theodore, Bede wrote his fascinating *History of the English Church and People*. He dedicated it to the king of Northumbria, Ceolwulf, a not particularly distinguished potentate. Bede sees the English people as already single and yet recognises that a little before they had been but a group of Germanic tribes, Jutes, Saxons, Angles, and even these three became divided into a larger number of local kingdoms within Britain. Bede is writing primarily an ecclesiastical history but it is for him also the history of a people, already a single people, though not a single state. The Church and the People here precede the state. When England gained a unifying monarchy and became a single state in the ninth and tenth centuries, the archbishopric of Canterbury and the church had already been functioning as a unifying factor for two centuries, even if the establishment of a second archbishopric at York in the mid-eighth century—something of a sop to Northumbrian nationalism—had diminished just a little the symbolic and administrative unity of the English church out of which emerge that of the English state.

As the kingdom of England develops in subsequent centuries to become the most compact and self-conscious state of western Europe in the central middle ages, the role of the archbishops of Canterbury remained politically a unique one. In many African peoples one finds a recognised spiritual power older than that of the monarch, an ancient authority belonging to some representative of the land and its people and required to validate subsequent government. Such in its own way in the relationship of primate to monarch was the case of England. Again, the very location of the see of Canterbury had its importance. Pope Gregory when he laid down, in writing to Augustine, his plans for the new church of England sensibly enough placed the southern archbishopric in London, for London was already well known to be the central city of this island, its commercial capital. But Augustine settled in Canterbury close to the court of his convert king, Ethelbert of Kent, and it never seemed to his successors appropriate to move, though any weight to the kingdom of Kent soon disappeared. And they were wise to remain there. Again, a subtle national symbolic balance was thereby created, expressing geographically a certain distance between the authority of the church upon the one hand, government and trade upon the other. A third strand to the special role of the archbishopric of Canterbury in national life relates to the fact that England was quite outside the vague borders of the Carolingian and Holy Roman Empire within which the sublime myth of the unity of Rome was resurrected in the west to imply a universal unity of the church with a single state. Such an implication of unity had been dangerous for the church in the fourth and fifth centuries and it was again dangerous now. Much of western Christendom as a whole—Spain for instance, as well as England—was effectively committed to a pluralism of monarchies as against a single empire. This inevitably diminished the mystique of the ruler and the scope for a politically-based monism, which always required in principle a geographical identity between church and state. But England cherished a particularly clear conviction that it was in no way within the empire. This both contributed to the rejection of the myth of monism and undergirded the quite special political position of Canterbury as primatial see in regard to this non-imperial kingdom.

Post-Carolingian western Christendom was, all the same, in England or elsewhere naturally monist. We see this, at its very best, in Alfred. The papacy was exceptionally weak: Rome was a city of pilgrimage with huge symbolic authority but almost none administratively. As northern European societies grew into Christianity and feudalism, kings appointed bishops unquestioned—good kings appointed holy monks, less good kings appointed their ten-year-old bastard sons. Alfred twice visited Rome on pilgrimage but his appointment of bishops was, surely, in the context of his age uncriticisable. William the Conqueror in the late eleventh century was, from this point of view, still a good king, but one of the last of his age. Lanfranc, his choice for Canterbury, was also one of the ablest of archbishops. They understood and respected one another well, almost too well. An Italian and a lawyer as well as a monk and a theologian, Lanfranc was certainly no mere servant of the king. Yet, more than at any previous point in English history, we may detect here—not by default but by deliberation—a shift away from the implicit dualism of the age of Theodore or even Dunstan towards a more Constantinian model—and William was not unlike Constantine in his sense of divine mission to order both church and state, though he had in Lanfranc a more equal partner than Constantine ever enjoyed.

The 'Gregorian' reform of the church from the eleventh century involved a good many things. From our point of view the most important was that it constituted a dualist reaction from the feudalist monism which had largely taken over the western church in the previous centuries. Gregory VII and his successors were reasserting the necessity of a critical distance between church and state even within a society which was, nominally, overwhelmingly Christian. The importance of this was accepted by English clerics of the twelfth and thirteenth centuries quite as much as by the church leadership in Rome or elsewhere. Yet undoubtedly, in England as more widely in the west, as the middle ages advanced with the growing secular confidence of princely rulers upon the one hand, the growing claims of canon law, the clerical order and the papacy upon the other, the relationship between church and state would become in theory increasingly problematic, being subject to the claims of two polarised, and finally equally unacceptable, monist models: systematic royal control upon the one hand, a high Gregorian view of an international church, wholly subject to the papacy and functioning as a clericalist and theocratic society, in final control of the lay world around it, upon the other. In his famous letter, Pope Gelasius divided the two swords but his successors seven centuries later were claiming them both. In the eleventh and twelfth centuries the threat to dualism came from the state, but by the thirteenth it came, in theory at least, in the claims of Innocent III and Boniface VIII, more from the church. But for a while, neither was quite to be realised.

I suspect that almost the last time in which in this country, in medieval circumstances, the old relationship of an involvement neither dominating nor dominated, but always deeply involved, is really to be seen—and then precariously—is in the archiepiscopate of Stephen Langton.

On 7 July 1220, fifty years after his murder, the body of Thomas Becket was translated with immense solemnity to a magnificent new shrine behind the choir of Canterbury Cathedral. Archbishop Langton had, like Becket, endured years of exile at the abbey of Pontigny. Now he was able to put the final touches to the canonisation of Thomas of London, the martyr-hero of the church's freedom. Upon Stephen's seal the martyrdom of Thomas was depicted. He was able to see himself as Thomas's heir, the archbishop in whose time the freedom of the church from undue royal control, for which Thomas had died, was now substantially accepted.

Langton was, nevertheless, about as different a person as could be imagined from Becket. The latter had been an impossibly flamboyant and egotistical actor, self-righteous and aggressive, a man of exceptional practical ability but rather little wisdom, someone all his life given to extremes: 'He was always a fool and always will be', growled his leading ecclesiastical enemy, Gilbert Foliot, Bishop of London, at one moment of crisis. It is hard quite to disagree and hard to sympathise with many of the specific issues he committed himself to so fiercely in his struggle with Henry II. Yet he was indeed struggling for the freedom of the church at a critical moment when the Gregorian programme to diminish lay control had been gaining ground in England for a generation under Thomas's predecessor at Canterbury, the great Theobald, but was now challenged by Henry's determination to maintain that control at least at the rather high level achieved by William I. Doubtless many of Thomas's immediate sticking points seem questionable yet the long years of his struggle with Henry, his martyrdom in the cathedral, canonisation and rapid transformation into one of the most popular saints of his time made of St Thomas a crucial symbol for the necessary freedom of the church, of its contemporary ability to maintain a critical distance from the crown, instead of being further domesticated as just a useful, because more educated, branch of the feudal and royal system. And such a symbol was what the far more temperamentally pacific Langton all the same needed.

Stephen appears, especially for a medieval archbishop, a singularly unostentatious person, not at all given to flamboyant poses. He had been a learned—but not too subtle or original—professor of theology in Paris until Innocent III made him a Cardinal and then proposed him in 1207 as Archbishop of Canterbury at a moment when King John and the Canterbury monks were in conflict over the election. It was an excellent choice. The monks accepted it but not John. Innocent laid the country under an interdict in consequence and Stephen took up residence at Pontigny. We must pass over most of the complex developments of the following years. John's increasingly difficult situation—the threat of French invasion, papal deposition, unrest at home—prompted him at last in 1212 to make his peace with the church and accept Langton as archbishop. It also prompted him in an excess of obsequious servility, to surrender England to the Pope to be held in future as a papal fief—an extraordinary move the idea of which most probably originated in England rather than in Rome but which Langton nevertheless described as something 'to be detested throughout the ages' (he was a loyal cardinal but hardly an ultramontane!). In consequence of all this the history of church-state relations in England for the next ten years was exceptionally complex, involving an unusual measure of papal intervention, but one of its most constant threads was that of the exceptionally balanced, but rather unaggressive, sense of responsibility of the Primate. It would seem to have been he who turned Magna Carta from being an expression of reactionary baronial factionalism into a genuinely national document, a very watermark of our constitutional history. It did, moreover, include as its first clause the immortal words 'that the English Church should be free'—'Quod Anglicana Ecclesia libera sit, et habeat jura sua integra, et libertates suas illaesas', including freedom of election (though, in fact, explicit reference to the latter was omitted from later re-issues of the charter). Langton was at this period both the king's adviser and yet not unsympathetic to the cause of the rebellious barons. When Innocent, now backing the king his vassal, quashed the charter, Stephen was unable to concur, was suspended in consequence and again left the country.

What is striking about Langton is how consistently low-keyed he seems to have been in relation to pope, king, barons, alike and yet how clear-mindedly his eyes were set upon the common good of church and state. In due course he returned to England, crowned Henry III, translated the relics of Thomas of Canterbury, held an influential national synod for the reform of the church in the wake of the fourth Lateran Council and obtained in 1225 a solemn reissue of the Charter. The pressures of both crown and papacy are clear enough in his life. He was in no way opposed to either institution though he could judge the behaviour of each at times unwise. But in his career as archbishop Stephen stands emphatically for the essential freedom of the church *vis à vis* the state, but never an irresponsible or over-clericalised freedom. He may be seen in this as the heir to Theodore, Dunstan and Theobald. The English church through most of the thirteenth century continued broadly on the same lines: many of its episcopal elections appear free, its bishops could on occasion stand up to both king and pope. They were pastors of weight and theologians rather than royal officials. St Edmund of Abingdon, Langton's near successor at Canterbury and another distinguished academic, appears as independent as Stephen. In his time and for a while afterwards a critical distance is still recognisable between spiritual and political power. Nevertheless that distance had long been threatened and was increasingly being lost. From the fourteenth century there would be few bishops of any significance who were not quite plainly the king's nominees and whose experience did not consist largely in government service. Behind the tenuous freedom of the church of Langton's age lay the powerful pastoral and canonical arm, acting a bit arrogantly at times, but still often genuinely helpful, of the papacy. Effectively from the period of the Avignon captivity that was lost and the establishment began; the almost complete subjugation of the church by the secular power, a pragmatic, untheoretical Constantinianism. The inherent perils of a Christendom in which church and society were too closely dovetailed were comfortably swallowing the freedom of *Ecclesia Anglicana*.

Pilgrims might continue in their multitude to the shrine of St Thomas at Canterbury but the point had been lost. In Langton's time it could appear that Thomas rather than Henry had won, a century later the opposite was clear enough and when Henry VIII smashed Becket's shrine three centuries later, he was only confirming the *status quo* by reversing the symbolism of that day in 1220 when Langton, fresh from crowning the young Henry III, had first set forth in all its splendour for the veneration of the people of England and as the politest of warnings to the English crown, the shrine of the martyred archbishop, a symbol of the critical distance needed between church and state.

Chapter Two

The Triumph and Decline of Justinianism

The thrust of the argument of the first chapter was that the New Testament, while in no way providing Christianity with a single normative pattern of church-state relations, does include a commitment to what we may call 'dualism' which the church can never safely renege upon. This was easily enough accepted when Christians formed but a minute sect or when, by the third century, they constituted a considerable but still minority community. However, once the minority became a majority and included the rulers themselves, the retention of an adequate distance between church and state became far more problematic, something requiring ceaseless vigilance if it was not only too easily to be lost. In the fourth century the very speed of change left Christians quite unprepared intellectually and institutionally for the problems now bound to arise and the inevitable pressure to move from dualism towards monism: the incorporation of church and state, each into other, such as to produce either—occasionally and fairly temporarily—a theocracy or, far more generally, an erastian subordination of the church to political authority. The more a large majority of people, perhaps literally almost everyone in a country, belongs to and has for generations belonged to, a single community of religious belief and ritual, the more difficult it is to avoid this outcome: a unified Christian society, combining church and state in an integrated organism, whereby the church's extraterritorial links are minimised and its Durkheimian role *vis à vis* this particular state becomes fundamental. A functioning pastoral integration of church and society inevitably stimulates, even if it does not actually command, a formal integration at the institutional level of church and state.

The more church and society appear coterminous, at least locally, the more the church is seen in terms of ordinary human life as a compulsory association, the more the cultural life of society is impregnated with a particular set of religious beliefs and practices, the more the state may feel almost compelled to regulate religion for the sake of the stability and accepted moral norms of the society for which it provides political leadership.

If it is of the nature of Christianity at its most characteristic to be significantly distinct from the state, then it should be vitally important for the church not only not to back up this sort of argumentation but actually to challenge it both theoretically and practically, including—where possible—the factual grounds for it. The presence of Jews in medieval society did in fact almost always mean that the church was not absolutely coterminous with the local human community. The determination to treat them as coterminous inevitably made the position of the Jews always more unpleasant until they were simply driven out—as from England at the end of the thirteenth century. At its best in the person, for instance, of Hugh of Lincoln, the medieval church did do something to protect the Jews but for the most part it did, of course—even and most regrettably at the high theological level of a Thomas Aquinas—go along with a view which wholly marginalised the non-Christian (and the non-Catholic) and justified highly abusive treatment. Far from defending the acceptability of pluralism, the medieval church handed on to almost all its chief immediate heirs the principle that religious non-conformity is unacceptable for either church or state, and that both should use the most dire means to extirpate it. As the middle ages progressed, the means had grown worse and worse. It may be that in some cases and to some degree this really is the duty of the state, but it certainly is not the right or duty of the church, and in so far as it was accepted as right, Christianity was being reduced to the level of a tribal religion or imperial cult (all that it had originally claimed most absolutely not to be) and its inherent exigency to be unmitigatedly universalist in regard to humanity was dramatically lost. Full legal establishment within a particular political society was simply an extreme form of the far wider europeanisation of Christianity. While on the one side in its positive dimension this expressed the particularist and incarnationalist thrust of Christianity, upon the other when a single type of incarnationalisation turned monopolistic, it was bound to undermine the larger claim to a potential total catholicity.

In the work of Justinian in the sixth century we have the Christian *locus classicus* for this solution, the culmination of the Constantinian process, a system which will be, ever after, the almost normative pattern for the Greek east but one which will also be imitated in the west by Charles the Great and the subsequent apologists for the Holy Roman Empire among many others. It is clear that in this, as in almost all areas of life, the tradition of Jesus was so open and structurally indeterminate that church history has been able to include almost every conceivable shaping of church-state relations. One cannot exclude Justinian and Charles the Great from Christian history, to say the least. And yet. The most profound inner logic of the gospel seems somewhere to have got lost in such a system—both the non-political freedom of Jesus and his church, and the ability actually to be creatively critical of the totality of life, including the political. That which a Christian society most needs politically from the church, that the Establishment Church must fail to give it. Succumbing to the temptation of incorporation into Caesar's establishment with all the resultant religious opportunities as well as temporal perks has deprived it of the pearl of great price. In the west this did not happen to the extent that it did in the east. If it did not, this was due partly to the legacy of Augustine and partly to the strength of the papacy which ensured the survival of a dualistic model and so made possible in principle a far more international and intercultural shaping for the church. It should even have worked for a more tolerant approach to outsiders. The Justinianic model of one church-one state hardly left room for any of this and almost inevitably produced in Egyptians, Syrians and what have you a great willingness to escape from a monistic church-empire, even into the arms of Islam. In uniting church with state so closely it will always and inevitably exclude from the church those not subject to the state, just as it will exclude from at least full membership of the state those not belonging to the church. It leads not only to the state's denial of a pluralist world but to the church's withdrawal from the sense of being a multi-national and multi-cultural fellowship and to settling instead for being Greek, German or English. However, the declining political power of Byzantium in subsequent centuries impeded the working out of such consequences in relation to the Slavs, especially the Russians, and effectively converted a universalist erastianism into a nationalist one.

Something of the same happened in the west. In its less central areas, being part of the One Catholic Church and part of Christian society did not mean in any way acknowledging the supremacy of the Holy Roman Emperor. There could be one church and a multiplicity of kingdoms. It was not, however, easy to resist monism's tempting theory or rather workable practice in the western medieval world, and some who did resist proceeded so to over-react as little by little to move to an alternative extreme and transform the particular episcopal ministry of the papacy into a theocratic and monist rival to the Empire, claiming the power of the secular sword for itself on the grounds of the so-called Donation of Constantine, or whatever, and functioning— for all the high words about the apostles—in a rather secularised administrative and jurisdictional manner. Gregory VII was right enough in realising the extreme urgency of liberating the church from almost total feudalism but—however much, in terms of his time, it may have been a near inevitable way of reacting—he becomes a far less sure guide for the future, when he develops instead a model of the church as a sort of separate international clerical empire of its own, claiming the power of the secular state as available at its final command, though functioning for the most part through legal control of the clergy alone. Both the spiritual power and the temporal possessions of the church in a medieval society were such that it was equally inevitable a prince should wish to control it as much as he could—control not only a bishop's use of his castles and the military strength of his vassals but also his capacity to excommunicate, to bind and to loose. Maybe only a centralised politicisation of the church's ministry, as attempted by the popes from the eleventh to the fourteenth century, could possibly have restrained the urge to erastianise the church in a feudal context, but it was done at an increasingly high price. The papacy's immediate objective became more and more reduced in practice to secure the political independence of its base in central Italy and sufficient money from elsewhere to pay for its burgeoning bureaucracy. Quite apart from the morals or statesmanlike sagacity of individual popes, the papacy itself simply became as time went on a less and less credible, lovable, imaginative image and instrument of what the Kingdom of God might conceivably signify.

What I have been suggesting, however, is that the English church did actually do not too bad a job of imaging the Kingdom while avoiding monist pretensions from the time of Theodore to the time of Langton—always of course fallible and peccable enough, yet beneath it credible all the same, and it did it largely through maintaining a critical distance from the state without being either unworldly or too much of an independent political power of its own. It retained something of the sense of pastoral priority, so stressed in Gregory the Great's *Cura Pastoralis* (a work which, when translated by King Alfred, became the first piece of English prose literature and is therefore to be seen as, from several viewpoints, a truly foundation document for English Christianity). Of course, one can easily exaggerate such a claim and find instances which don't fit with it at all well. One can focus instead on plenty of highly 'royal' episcopal appointments in every century. The ideal was certainly seldom achieved, but it was also not entirely lost and—in the life of the church—that is about the best one is ever likely to manage in any sphere of things.

But from the fourteenth century we seem to move steadily down the track away from 'not entirely lost'. While the immediate resistance to high papal and canonical pretensions could be expressed in dualist terms (and really was, for instance, at the Council of Merton in 1236 and Bracton's defence of English customary law against Grosseteste's insistence upon its alteration to conform to canon law) in practice what resulted was less a balance than a new erastianisation. Centralised papalisation of the church's official functioning—run efficiently enough but, all the more absurdly, from Avignon—actually helped erode the case for genuine ecclesiastical freedom at a local level and in point of fact handed over the *Ecclesia Anglicana* with next to no protest to effective local state control. Practical admission of this in the fourteenth and fifteenth centuries was transformed into theoretical assertion in the sixteenth. This led on to a quiet mopping up operation in the seventeenth and eighteenth to ensure that no voice of the church, distinct from that of the state and the ruling classes, could possibly function. England could then be seen as a little local model of the principle of establishment, of the Justinianic Church. It was justified primarily in terms of its being self-evidently right, secondarily in terms of the horrors of Rome, upon the one hand, and—when necessary—those of Geneva upon the other.

The explosion of the Reformation was not, by any means, just a new twist to church-state relations. It was an explosion precipitated by the altered possibilities of religion and scriptural exegesis in a world of printing, by a deep sense of moral repudiation of much of church government as it had come to be carried on, by the sheer requirement of all living religion to make from time to time a fresh start, uncluttered by the bric-à-brac left over by the devotions of the past. The church-state relationship was, indeed, often but a channel through which these great forces moved. In England the *real politic* of Thomas Cromwell and Henry VIII could both use and be used by religious unrest. Together they turned the quasi-royal establishment of the previous period, already streamlined by the short-sighted regime of Cardinal Wolsey, into one of total royal control.

Listen to the decisive words of the Act in Restraint of Appeals of February 1533:

> That this Realm of England is an Empire and so hath been accepted in the world, governed by one supreme head and king, having the dignity and royal estate of the imperial crown of the same, unto whom a body politic compact of all sorts and degrees of people divided in terms and by names of spirituality and temporality, to be bounded and ought to

bear, also institute and furnished, by the goodness and sufferance of Almighty God, with plenary, whole, and entire power, preeminence, authority, prerogative and jurisdiction . . .

Despite the creeping erastianism of late medieval England this was still revolutionary and William Warham, the Archbishop of Canterbury, had asserted a little before that 'It were indeed as good to have no spirituality as to have it at the prince's pleasure'. But Warham was now dead and his successor Thomas Cranmer, the principal religious mind behind England's new church order, was a total erastian by conviction. He was the last person to be able to modify theologically the politically-motivated Justinianism of king and minister.

Justinian's concept of the single empire, spiritual and temporal, ruled by its supreme head, the emperor, is here transferred to the national state and it will, in due course, be effectively transferred to every petty German princeling: *cuius regio, eius et religio*. Dangerous enough in relation to a great empire centring on the New Rome and claiming a Christian universality stretching in Justinian's time across Italy and North Africa, Egypt and Syria as well as the Greek-speaking lands around Constantinople, it becomes extraordinarily absurd when applied to Wurtemburg or Hesse, but—at least in retrospect—not much less so when applied to England. Yet in an age of poor communications a fairly centralised island kingdom of not inconsiderable extent was a natural socio-political context for the assertion of Justinianic principles.

In theory Thomas More and John Fisher could protest, with sound ecclesiastical reason and the consensus over many centuries of the whole western church, at the rejection of a papal authority which had been unquestioned in England since the foundation of the see of Canterbury, but they did, of course, hardly if at all question the kind of integrated relationship between church and state which had been taken for granted nearly as long and which, in its later development and realist political terms, had led only too inevitably to this dénouement. Nor, when for years they had lived within a church-state regime controlled by Wolsey, Archbishop of York, Cardinal and Papal Legate, but always the king's servant first and last, had they so much in practice to offer as an alternative. They would, doubtless, have liked and prayed for a purified church—purified as much in Rome as in England—but they could hardly have envisaged a purification delving deep into theology and canon law, yet nothing less could possibly have held back the tides either of Reformation doctrine or state absolutism. What the English church was actually landed with was a none too purifying revolution, which wholly eliminated one of the problems but at the price of much accentuating the other.

Meanwhile the Catholic church in France or Spain sank almost as completely beneath the power of the sovereign, though it did theoretically retain a more than national institutional authority to sustain some hint of the church's catholicity, freedom and otherness from Caesar. In the Calvinist system, there was far more. Despite the somewhat theocratic character of Geneva, an inherent dualism and distinction of church and state was better preserved—some measure of freedom for the church to speak its mind to the state—than it was in Lutheranism or Anglicanism. And that tradition of freedom was passed on to Scotland and has always remained there. On this issue the true Protestant can agree with the true Catholic against the erastian. As Forsyth, best of the Free Church theologians writing in the late Victorian era, declared (*Rome, Reform and Reaction, 1899, p 24*):

> At the English Reformation there were but the two alternatives—a royal Church or a Roman Church, Erastianism or Catholicism. If you resented the royal supremacy you could realize the freedom of the Church only in a Catholic form, and between Henry and More our heart is all with More.

It was Richard Hooker who did more than anyone else to canonise and render defensible the theory behind the Act in Restraint of Appeals in his *Laws of Ecclesiastical Polity* written in the 1590s. As a theologian Hooker was a traditionalist deeply indebted to Thomas Aquinas and this has helped to obscure the fact that his concept of the relationship of church and state was not, in the fullest sense, traditional. Grounded in the Old Testament rather than the New, it gently but firmly rejected dualism. He who has supreme power in the state can also have it, most fittingly, within the Christian church.

> There is not any man of the Church of England but the same man is also a member of the commonwealth; nor any man a member of the commonwealth, which is not also of the Church of England. (Eccl Pol VIII i.2)

Here is the Anglican ideal: the identity of church and state led by its monarch. The Christian sovereigns Hooker quotes were, unsurprisingly, Constantine and Justinian (Eccl Pol V, lxi.2; lxxx.6). Hooker's vision is so satisfying for the moderate nationalist, his tone so judicious, his style so elegant that even into the twentieth century it has been hard for Anglicans to recognise that it was a misleading vision, neither theologically nor factually well grounded.

It took people a long time to begin to see what really was wrong. The central religious and political conflicts of this country in the seventeenth century were still far more about just what kind of church was to be imposed by the state than about the inherent nature of the relationship between the two. Nevertheless in practice the Civil War and its aftermath slowly forced more and more people to a recognition that *cuius regio eius religio* was an unacceptable principle for Christian reasons while total religious uniformity was ceasing to be a practical or useful objective for the state. Too many 'members of the commonwealth' obstinately refused to be 'also of the Church of England' as by the crown constituted. Oliver Cromwell was probably the first of our rulers to edge towards a new model involving a major relaxation of the bonds of state and church, while the reactionary Tories of Charles II's Restoration made one last attempt to reimpose them. Hence John Bunyan wrote part I of *Pilgrim's Progress* in Bedford Gaol, imprisoned for illegal preaching. Tories could be outraged by the papistically inclined tolerance of the Stuart Declarations of Indulgence, but to some extent at least those Declarations did reflect the vision of William Penn, founder of the Quaker-inspired state of Pennsylvania and more than anyone else in that period the prophet of a new deal in church-state relations. Part II of *Pilgrim's Progress*, published late in Charles II's reign, reflects a nonconformist ministry already functioning. When William and Mary ousted her father James they could not wholly go back on that new wind of toleration. Something of a new deal was bound to come, though the Toleration Act of 1689 was not exactly generous in its lines. English society was pragmatically recognised to exist on a religiously two-tier basis: first-class citizens, who were Anglicans; various degrees of second-class citizens, who were everyone else. The latter were now to be permitted to survive quietly in peace so long as they could put up with a good deal of discrimination and be almost totally excluded from the political community. Such would be the state of things until the upheavals of the nineteenth century. The public challenge to establishment might seem slight but the logic of Hooker was already abandoned.

The internal erastianisation of the Church of England was itself a lengthy process. Just as it did not begin with Henry VIII, so it did not end with him. The bishops of the next hundred years retained individually at least as much spark of freedom as their predecessors of the fifteenth century and they were theologically more informed men. Perhaps Laud may be seen as the last medieval archbishop of Canterbury, medieval not only in prelatical arrogance but in a certain independent use of his position for the public good. From the late seventeenth century erastianism takes a tighter and tighter grip upon almost all the processes of the church, but the case of the Non-Jurors remains both paradoxical and illuminating. The high churchmen of Restoration England had added to the practice of erastianism a particular loathing of rebellion linked with the doctrine of the Divine Right of Kings and renewed each year in the Prayer Book liturgy appointed to be said on January 30, the day of Charles I's execution, and May 29, the day of Charles II's restoration. In these prayers a high erastianism holding together church and legitimacy was emphatically asserted.

Yet England was not an absolute monarchy and churchmen had to combine their royalism with due respect for a parliamentary constitution. In the case of men like Archbishop Sancroft and Bishop Ken it had also to be combined with a particularly sensitive conscience. So loyal were they that a Roman Catholic head of a Protestant church was not at first admitted to be a problem. But James II managed to demonstrate that you may not be able to square the circle even with the piety of a Sancroft. Upon the one hand the bishops found themselves unable to obey the king and read his unconstitutional Declaration of Indulgence on account of which James, with incredible foolishness, put them on trial. Upon the other they were unable to go along with James's deposition and the accession of William and Mary which ran counter to all their Tory theory. They could accept neither royal tyranny nor its overthrow by *realpolitik.* In consequence the Archbishop of Canterbury and five of his colleagues were deprived on royal authority. What had happened was that a low pragmatic erastianism had prevailed—as it must—over a high theoretical and romantic erastianism. The spirituality of establishment had been revealed at its finest but also least practical. The Vicar of Bray's final affirmation of loyalty was that 'George my lawful king shall be, until the times do alter'. In a sense almost everyone may be inclined to go along with this, but for a church clinging to a principled erastianism it can be just that much more awkward. A little before the Fall of Constantinople its patriarch had written to the Grand Duke of Moscow that 'It is not possible for christians to have a church and not to have an emperor'. Yet ecclesiastical life had to go on and after the Fall its patriarch received his insignia of office from the Turkish Sultan instead. A mystical erastianism had departed to leave mere dependence upon the secular power. What had happened in the case of the Non-Jurors symbolised too the shift for the church from royal supremacy to parliamentary supremacy, a shift which simply reflected the development of English government but which would all the more undermine any basic logic in the system when parliament was opened to Scottish Presbyterians with the Act of Union and—in the nineteenth century—to anyone. Just as the Orthodox emperor could turn into a Muslim Sultan so a 'Protestant Parliament' might conceivably turn into an assembly of Roman Catholics, Nonconformists, atheists, Muslims and Jews. The Hookerian theory had wholly ceased to work, yet continued to retain for devout establishment minds a residue of seductive power.

The Non-Jurors of 1689 followed the Baptists, the Presbyterians, the Quakers and the Catholics into the silence of disestablishment. But, in truth, the establishment itself could be hardly less silent. The Convocations ceased to function. The archbishops, while keeping ducal state at Lambeth Palace, almost ceased to have anything to do with Canterbury Cathedral, the see of their teaching. The eighteenth-century church was by no means devoid of piety, learning and pastoral care, but its leadership had lost any sense of distance from the governing elite, while at every level of society the clergy were assimilated more than ever to the gentry. It was an intensely domesticated church and even its more pious bishops tended to judge appointments almost wholly in terms of income and status. The very toleration granted the Free Churches had taken pressure off the establishment, while the condition of the Free Churches did not engender in them either a new approach to the church-state relationship. It merely left them rather apolitical. Pietism was the characteristic spirituality of the eighteenth century. It was the opposite side of the coin to erastianism. The Whig state had reduced religion to political inconsequence.

With the nineteenth century the whole picture very quickly changes. The Free Churches multiply and are repoliticised across the media of the Liberal and Labour parties; the union with Ireland made Catholicism once more numerically and politically significant. Facts determine theory or, at least, they undermine bad theory. Just as, in the seventh, eighth or ninth century, monism was largely excluded by the fact that the one church coincided geographically with not one but many monarchies, so now monism was undermined by the more and more obvious fact that the state coincided geographically with many churches. At the same time secular liberalism challenged the whole idea of confessional privilege, until even Anglicans began to recognise the disadvantages of governmental control. It is ironic that the establishment was decreed in the sixteenth century in terms of 'Empire' because it was exactly when Britain really did become an empire that erastianism manifestly ceased to work: the empire could only function politically across the world on a basically pluralistic religious model. Far from justifying erastianism, the reality of empire required it to be dished. Establishment had to be quietly transmogrified into what third-century Christians had been asking for before Constantine had set the establishment experiment going: a free church in a neutral state. However, while in this country the Free Churches and Roman Catholics were naturally running with the current of this transition (a current to which society itself was now decisively committed), most Anglicans equally naturally still struggled to hold it back as much as possible.

Doubtless the third-century model was hardly considered, but the American model could not so easily be ignored. There were ambiguities within the American experience. New England origins are largely to be found within quite explicit intolerance of a Protestant sort; even the Catholic-inspired colony of Maryland, first of all English-speaking societies to pass an Act of religious toleration, had for a while turned to proscribing Catholics. The established Church of England was relatively weak in America and in pre-Independence days never had the foresight to set up even one diocese. The United States had no alternative to one of total separation between church and state, even if some had slight qualms at first about fully extending its freedoms to Catholics. As immigrants poured in from every part of Europe during the nineteenth century and from every ecclesiastical tradition, the separation of church and state remained obviously essential. While the significance of this for England was probably not felt to be considerable at the beginning of the century, by the second half its message was clear enough. In America the churches were flourishing and the state flourished too without controlling them. Here was an English-speaking and largely Protestant world in which establishment was unthinkable. The heart of 'Americanism', which was proving attractive to Roman Catholics too, was a free church in a free state and by 1900 it was making any alternative European pattern look distinctly anachronistic.

The battle for the establishment, in any strong form, had really been lost long before that. Sir Owen Chadwick opens his great two-volume history of the Victorian Church with a very detailed account of Catholic Emancipation in 1829. He was right to do so because Catholic Emancipation both largely caused and best symbolised the manifest collapse of the old system, though in the long run the requirements of both secular liberalism and Nonconformity (freed from disability one year before, 1828) were no less decisive. But Catholic Emancipation was more shocking to the traditional mind and more immediate in its implications. While for a century and more the British state had tolerated the existence of non-Anglicans, it was really only as mice in the woodwork, beings whose presence could hardly be justified in terms of public doctrine and who had, then, to be excluded from anything of real importance. Scottish Presbyterians were to be treated as honorary Anglicans while Scottish Episcopalians and the discrimination they suffered had to be conveniently forgotten. That was indeed an anomaly but as, to the popular and lay mind, the stress was upon 'Protestant' not 'Anglican' in terms of the official religion of England, it seemed not too great an anomaly. But then, in 1800, it was decided by England's rulers that Ireland should be united in parliament with England and a little later—due to Daniel O'Connell—it became abundantly clear that unless Irish Catholics could be elected to parliament, Ireland would be ungovernable. So they were and from that moment on a Roman Catholic might be Prime Minister. Parliament, the country's supreme authority, ceased in principle to be Protestant. While everything was done to play down the religious implications of this for England, in fact in 1829 imperial *raison d'état* ended the establishment in any coherent form. Everything subsequent was but a mopping up operation, as bit by bit surviving privileges of the Church of England were cut away, grievances of non-Anglicans remedied.

The psychological shock of living in a society where the state no longer controlled the church was brought home far more in 1850 than in 1829. Rome restored the Catholic hierarchy in England and headed it by an Archbishop of Westminster. Cardinal Wiseman made matters worse by a singularly bombastic pastoral issued 'from out the Flaminian Gate' certain to upset Protestant susceptibilities. No place name is more central to the British establishment than Westminster and to have an Archbishop of Westminster, not appointed by the British crown yet spiritual leader of millions of British citizens, was the exact contradiction to what the church's establishment had meant. It was certainly a bold move to choose the title of Westminster and not some innocuous locality such as Hounslow or Croydon (given that the titles of existing Anglican sees were excluded by law). I cannot help feeling that it was also a very shrewd one. It was proof positive that English Catholics, as well as Irish Catholics, were not going to behave any more as mice in the woodwork.

John Keble's famous assize sermon on National Apostasy in 1833 had represented a cry of high Tory agony responding to a sense of betrayal as it recognised where erastianism was taking the church in a more liberal age. Of course it was misguided both in what it could not stomach (the abolition of some Irish bishoprics) and in what it had stomached for so long. But the conclusion of the Tractarian movement was a right one: rediscover a sense of the church as independent with a nature of its own, free of state control, a voice of its own. The practical crumbling of establishment inevitably forced thoughtful churchmen to rethink the whole relationship of church and state, but this led them to very varied conclusions. Let us consider four of the strongest religious personalities of the age: Thomas Arnold, William Gladstone, John Henry Newman and Henry Manning. The oldest of the four was Arnold, born in 1795, the youngest Gladstone in 1809. As Arnold died young, in 1842, fifty years before the other three, he may not seem to fit well with them yet he was essentially their contemporary. Famous for his remark that the Church of England as it then was 'no human power' could save, his response to the problem remained erastian: church and nation must remain one. As they are now very far from one, the Church of England should be reshaped on a still more comprehensive and almost wholly non-dogmatic basis so as to re-include everyone (except Roman Catholics, Quakers, Jews and atheists whom even Arnold saw could not be absorbed). Such a solution was wholly impractical but it expresses the only way a Hookerian model might theoretically be retained—and Arnold was a great admirer of Hooker: the nation needs an established moral dimension, such should be the church. Much of the rest of Hooker's theology was, inevitably, thrown overboard.

Of our four only Arnold died confident in the value of establishment. Gladstone, Newman and Manning, while all three deriving from a high church and Tory background, were each forced little by little to painful reappraisal. As a young man in 1838 Gladstone, still a Tory, defended the principle of a single state religion in *The State in its relations with the Church*. Thirty years later he would be the architect of Irish disestablishment and, as leader of the Liberal Party, he was forced increasingly to recognise the contemporary unreality of any deep principles underlying the continued establishment of a state church. The gap between the theory of establishment and the reality of a liberal pluralist society was simply too great. Yet as Prime Minister, despite his frequently asserted hatred of erastianism, he continued to operate a highly erastian system. It was his clerical friends Newman and Manning who moved most forthrightly and furthest. Newman long felt himself intensely a Tory and nostalgically he remained one to the end. He never became anti-establishment, his mind had simply concentrated on quite other, more doctrinal, issues and they took him out of the state church. In subsequent years he recognised clearly enough that the old Tory view of the unity of church and state was now an anachronism, but well beyond this recognition lay his very clear assertion of the rightness of dualism. The heart of his letter to the Duke of Norfolk in response to Gladstone in 1874 was the chapter on 'Divided Allegiance', the reconciliation in conscience of the claims of 'two authorities'.

But it was Manning for whom the rejection of establishment and the reasserting of a vigorous dualism became the decisive issue for his conversion and subsequent life. The Archdeacon of Chichester abandoned the Church of England and became a Catholic essentially on the issue of erastianism in the wake of the Gorham Judgement of 1850. He was moving in his own mind from a church ruled by the Judicial Committee of the Privy Council to one ruled by its bishops. Son of a Governor of the Bank of England, close Oxford friend of Gladstone, Manning was destined by background, education and temperament for the highest of offices. Theologically second rate, he was exceptionally clear-sighted in practical affairs and well able to recognise the essential anachronism of a state-controlled church in the mid-nineteenth-century world. As he could not, in consequence, be Archbishop of Canterbury he became Cardinal Archbishop of Westminster instead. But he did not abandon the English world of high power by doing so. Until 1870 he corresponded almost incessantly with Gladstone. He intervened in every sort of social issue, English and Irish. In 1889, in great old age, he successfully mediated in the London Dock strike. Next year in the May Day procession his portrait was carried on banners beside that of Karl Marx. In a wide sense Manning remained very much part of the British establishment despite the inevitable suspicions of such an ultramontane-minded cardinal in Victorian England. But he was politically independent. Here was an archbishop in the heart of London who had regained that necessary distance from Caesar which Samuel Wilberforce, Bishop of Oxford, his brother-in-law, or Archbishop Tait had not.

The Church of England in these circumstances more and more felt itself to have the worst of both worlds. It was controlled by the state but increasingly not protected by the state. When it came to the disestablishment of the Church of Ireland, Gladstone might pay more attention to the views of the Archbishop of Westminster than to those of the Archbishop of Canterbury. He had in fact in 1868 received his copy of Manning's pamphlet *Ireland, a Letter to Earl Grey*, just four days before announcing his commitment to disestablishment. No wonder that in the 1850s a growing group of clergy, backed by Bishop Wilberforce, forced the revival of Convocation—first of Canterbury, and then of York. It was the beginning of the long march to General Synod and to ensuring that in practice the church was sufficiently distant from the state to be able to speak its own mind when it needed to.

If the growth of the empire reduced, for the British Government, the significance of the established Church of England, it also made the Church of England think rather differently of itself. An early move in this direction derived from a very ending of empire: with the Independence of the United States, American Anglicans needed their own bishop and sent Samuel Seabury to England in the hope of obtaining his consecration. But the Church of England could hardly authorise the consecration of a bishop for rebels or indeed for anyone outside His

Majesty's dominions. The self-understanding of an erastian church did not go so far. Fortunately for the Americans there was also an episcopalian church in Scotland, by no means established. So Seabury went to Aberdeen and was consecrated bishop in November 1784 in an upper room. As the years went on, the number of bishops in communion with the church of England but not appointed by the Queen steadily increased: in Scotland and America, in Canada and Australia and after Irish disestablishment even in Ireland. The Anglican Communion was coming into existence. The first Lambeth Conference met in 1867 in which the bishops of England—at least those who agreed to attend (some, like the Archbishop of York, refused)—rubbed shoulders with A.N. Niagara and T. Barbados, with the Bishop of Argyll and the Isles, the Bishop of Tennessee, the Bishop of Alabama and lots of others, none of whom had any relationship to the state. The Lambeth Conference was only a consultative assembly, but it both represented and contributed to a profound psychological alteration going on in the relationship between Anglicans and the state, and just because they were no longer simply 'C of E' they were—as C of E—part of something larger, and that something larger was unestablished by the state. Ever since 1867, as Lambeth Conferences have met every ten years or so, the Anglican Communion has grown, while the Church of England has, proportionately, shrunk.

It would, however, be much mistaken to depict the Established Church of late Victorian times as a body which had lost its nerve, enslaved by the Judicial Committee of the Privy Council, bemoaning the advance of the disestablishment campaign from Ireland to Wales upon the one hand, the ultramontane populist aggression of Cardinal Manning at the heart of the capital upon the other, yet looking too a little wistfully at the green fields of unestablished Anglican churches multiplying from New Zealand to Louisiana. In fact, to the contrary, the late nineteenth century was in many ways a golden age for the establishment precisely as establishment. It benefited from reflecting the light of the staid moral glory of the Queen herself. The church always does seem to have benefited most from female sovereigns—Elizabeth, Anne, Victoria and, indeed, Elizabeth II. Perhaps appropriate ecclesiastical leadership of this sort comes more convincingly from women. The erastian control of the church was managed so much more conscientiously than in previous ages. Gone were the days of easy political appointments. In Queen Victoria the church had a model head, ever anxious to find the best bishops, quite willing to veto bad proposals and successful in insisting that Lambeth should at least be consulted by Downing Street before appointments were made. In prime ministers like Gladstone and

Salisbury it had pious churchmen for whom ecclesiastical patronage was a grave moral responsibility. It might be hard to think of a better practical way to get good appointments and, of course, many of the bishops of the time were outstanding. It was known that a few bishops were Liberals, most Tories, but the sense of party character had much diminished, and the success of Bishop Westcott of Durham as a mediator between miners and mine owners in 1892 showed that not only Manning could act independently in matters of social and political concern. Westcott had a reputation as a socialist—surely a very woolly sort of socialist. It did not stop Lord Salisbury from recommending him for Durham, though the 'socialist tendencies' of his speeches did make Salisbury reject the Queen's suggestion that he might be further promoted to York.

Randall Davidson, Archbishop of Canterbury from 1903 to 1928, represents best of all this last mellow phase of an establishment which had lost its underlying *raison d'état* but was trying all the harder to justify itself by the responsible sobriety of its behaviour. Archbishop Tait's son-in-law and chaplain and then Dean of Windsor and adviser to the Queen, no one was more wholly erastian by temperament, an erastian of the most conscientious sort, the ceaseless but always deferential counsellor of monarchs and prime ministers, completely at home in the House of Lords and in every corridor of the highest echelons of the secular establishment. Yet it was he who overcame his conservative instincts and the appeals of his high Tory friends to speak and vote for the Liberal Parliament Bill of 1910 at a time of high constitutional crisis. He would seem to have acted at that moment with the authority and final independence of a true primate, rising above party and personal preference to consider only the good of the nation. Again, in 1926, Davidson's message to the nation suggesting precise terms for the ending of the General Strike, while certainly in no way radical or directly supportive of the Strike, was yet sufficiently out of line with government policy for conservatives to be furious, working men to cheer him in the streets. Reith, Director General of the BBC, who would perhaps have liked to see himself as a sort of Archbishop of Canterbury of the new age, felt so unsure of his own position at that moment of crisis that he actually refused for several days to allow the Archbishop's message to be broadcast. It would, I believe, in the days of his father-in-law have been unimaginable for the Archbishop of Canterbury to take even so much an independent line. Of course, Davidson had by then been archbishop for nearly thirty years and had a quite exceptional standing, nationally and internationally. He had presided over the new Church Assembly, which first met in June 1920—half-way house from the

Convocations to General Synod in providing the church with a measure of self-government—and over two Lambeth Conferences, of 1908 and 1920. (He had been responsible for the publication of the records of all the Conferences from the start.) The role of an Archbishop had been internationalised in his lifetime. One feels in this Scotsman something of the range of 'cura pastoralis' of the sort we found in Theodore of Tarsus or Stephen Langton: an internationally-minded leader of *Ecclesia Catholica* rather than the senior bishop of an erastian church. The intimate, rather degrading, linkage with the state had not yet been lost—as the fiasco over the Prayer Book made clear—even though the need for greater freedom upon both sides was becoming clear too. Anachronistic as the parliamentary control over the liturgy and government control of the appointment of bishops now appeared, no one was yet quite willing to tackle it. As it was, the Abdication crisis, the First World War and the restorationist mood of the age of Geoffrey Fisher meant that the inevitable decisions to restore to the church an adequate measure of freedom could be put off another forty years. Yet they had become inevitable. Glorious as the establishment in some ways was in the days of Davidson—far more glorious than in earlier eras—one feels that it necessarily represented a precarious, unstable and temporary equilibrium. The relationship of church and state could function in the modern world on the model of Cardinal Manning, but it could not really function for long upon that of Archbishop Davidson.

Chapter Three

A Tradition of Dissent

> Remember, remember
> The Fifth of November
> Gunpowder, Treason and Plot.
> I see no reason
> Why Gunpowder Treason
> Should ever be forgot.

The point of remembering it was, of course, to keep well in everyone's mind the treacherous and anti-English character of Catholicism. If England has—or, rather, used to have—a national day comparable with the 14th of July in France or the 4th of July in the United States, then it was surely the 5th of November. The much reduced form of its celebration, the mere bonfire night or fireworks display, with no ideological content left to it, that remains all we have today does not at all reveal the 5th of November as it used to be until a couple of generations back. England never has had any other genuine national day. This one was at once official, liturgical and—above all—popular: a festivity which commemorated the supreme national liberation, even (in its mythology, including its academicised form, the 'Whig Interpretation of History') the very formation of the nation as it really is: Protestant and free. Two centuries of events were linked together in this saga of our English Exodus: the rejection of the papal stranglehold over our national church; the Marian martyrdoms, made so much more significant by Foxe's *Book of Martyrs*; Pope Pius V's excommunication and deposition of Elizabeth I; the defeat of the Spanish Armada; Gunpowder Plot itself; lastly, James II's attempt to recatholicise the English monarchy and his overthrow and replacement by William of Orange to ensure what has since remained part of the law of this land: the Protestant Succession. Remember that William actually landed at Torbay on the 5th of November and that the prayers commanded to be said on this day in the Book of Common Prayer would henceforth link the two events:

Gunpowder Plot in 1605 and the Orange Victory of 1688. The northern Irish Protestant has continued to celebrate this saga in the commemoration of its final episode, the Battle of the Boyne of July 1690. While this now appears almost incomprehensible to most English people, so ignorant have we become—perhaps mercifully—of our own historical culture, it is in fact but the final extension of a mythology which was English rather than Irish.

At every point this saga was an anti-Catholic and anti-Roman one. England in its religion, its parliament, its freedom, its commercial prosperity and political might is seen as emerging, a quintessentially Protestant state, through providential liberation from Roman tyranny:

> O God, whose Name is excellent in all the earth and thy glory above the heavens; who on this day didst miraculously preserve our Church and State from the secret contrivance and hellish malice of Popish conspirators; and on this day also didst begin to give us a mighty Deliverance from the open tyranny and oppression of the same cruel and bloodthirsty enemies: we bless and adore thy glorious Majesty, as for the former, so for this thy late marvellous loving kindness to our Church and Nation, in the preservation of our religion and liberties.

There is a fair foundation of truth behind this mythology if also, naturally enough, a good deal of pretty partisan interpretation. At its start, the notion of a medieval papal tyranny over the English church has been recognised by modern scholarship as a very one-sided view of a relationship in which the English church benefited greatly from Rome, especially in the earlier centuries. Even the Marian executions, dreadful as they were, were not so different from Henrician or Elizabethan executions, yet I would not myself discount their effect. They took place over quite a short period of time and were mostly of very ordinary people. Their impact upon the popular mind should not be underestimated, especially when linked through the Queen's marriage with the much disliked influence of Spain. But it was probably the papal deposition of Elizabeth in 1570, the massacre of Protestants in France only two years later on St Bartholomew's Day, and then the attempted invasion by Spain, the greatest Catholic power of the day, in the 1580s—an invasion backed by some English Catholic clerical leaders on the continent—which really established the Catholic Church as England's supreme moral enemy. If the Gunpowder Plot adds a uniquely vivid expression of what it was all thought to be about—a threat to the very survival of our constitutional 'liberties'—it was the events of the 1680s that finally drove home the message: here was James II, a Catholic, on the throne, and the immediate consequences of this, the trial of the seven bishops upon the one hand, the hasty intrusion of Catholics into all sorts of positions, including a Jesuit in the Privy Council, upon the other. France was now the great Catholic power and the nation's principal enemy, and James could appear as little more than Louis XIV's puppet. Moreover in 1685 Louis revoked the Edict of Nantes and unleashed a wave of persecution upon French Protestants vastly more ruthless than English Catholics had ever had to suffer.

The historic opposition between the English state and the Catholic Church could hardly seem more absolute and many English people have certainly felt it to be so. And yet it is not quite as simple as that. Let us consider first the Catholic Church as a community of English people, a small but rather distinguished minority who refused to abandon their country's pre-Reformation religious heritage or accept an erastian church, whatever the consequences. While there were among them a very few who would have welcomed a Spanish victory in the 1580s and a few more who were prepared to plot on their own an internal dynastic revolution (a good old English tradition anyway and one Protestants could very much share in too), there is no doubt of the deep loyalty of the English Catholic community as a whole to its Protestant rulers. There is no evidence whatever to suggest that many English Catholics were in any way opposed to parliamentary government, something deeply rooted in pre-Reformation history. Thomas More, always the archetype of the English Catholic ideal, was not only 'the King's good servant, but God's first', he had also been Speaker of the House of Commons. The new absolutist model of Catholic monarchy which had developed from the sixteenth century onwards may have been attractive in its court glitter to some aristocratic Catholic exiles on the continent. It was not at all what most English Catholics were striving for. St Henry Walpole, awaiting execution in prison, wrote that for 'good government' England had no comparison on earth. Sir Thomas Tresham, the very model of old-fashioned Catholic gentleman, who spent long years in prison but refused to bow to bullying from either queen or pope, declared that he would most willingly defend the realm against 'prince, pope or potentate'. I remember as a young man, educated in a home as devoutly Catholic as it was liberal, my sheer astonishment at reading Evelyn Waugh, in his Foreword to the autobiography of the Jesuit William Weston, remark 'It may seem to us now that for the fullest development of our national genius' the Spanish Armada should have succeeded. Only a very ultramontane convert could pretend to think like that! To a large extent Protestants recognised, at least at the local level, that

English Catholics were not really their enemies. Relations were usually much better than might be imagined from a study of either the penal laws or the Book of Common Prayer.

Small in number as they were, Catholics never acquired a sectarian mentality. They retained a strong sense of public responsibility and of still constituting in waiting the church of the nation. What their experience had forced them towards, and very interestingly, was recognition of the clear divide between religious obedience and political obedience—Thomas More, not perhaps surprisingly in being a lawyer of the common law who was also an amateur theologian, had already come to a precise recognition of the divide—difficult as this could still be made for them by Rome. Pius V's Bull represented a late, anachronistic, expression of papal monism. English Catholics were, in point of fact, exceptionally orthodox in relation to the *longue durée* of Catholicism in their quite explicit assertion of dualism. Nevertheless it required a quite mature theology to accept the core of Rome's spiritual claims so unswervingly while equally rejecting its temporal claims, and of course not every Catholic was as clear-minded as Tresham. Post-Reformation English Catholics had rejected erastianism to a degree that pre-Reformation Catholics seldom managed (Gardiner had been just as erastian as Cranmer). They did not thereby become sectarian in temperament or withdraw from society and political concerns any more than they were compelled to do.

Nor even was Rome itself nearly so anti-English as the national myth might suggest. The Popes had agonised for years over what to do about Elizabeth and were very far from being in full sympathy with Spanish or French imperialism. Indeed Innocent XI, the most outstanding of seventeenth-century popes, was in continual conflict with Louis XIV's absolutist claims and actually excommunicated Louis in secret in 1688, the year of James's overthrow. For Innocent, Louis was more or less a French Henry VIII who never went quite so far doctrinally. So, while it was by no means unreasonable for English Protestants to see Louis and his ally James as both a very real threat to the freedom and constitution of England and essentially a Catholic threat, the reality was more complex.

In consequence of all this England entered the modern age with a constitution and a national consciousness profoundly committed not only to Protestantism, but to an almost neurotic anti-Catholicism, yet also with a small, rather stoic, Catholic minority of the deepest loyalty and Englishness, almost over-compensating in both for its principled refusal to go along with the national church and for its consequent three centuries of penalisation. But at least by the latter half of the eighteenth century, as Britain's imperial power grew, government began increasingly to recognise the importance of accommodating Catholicism, in Bombay, Canada, Trinidad, as well as in Ireland and England. If it had given up the attempt wholly to banish the authority of Rome from England itself, it had still more failed to do so in Ireland and had soon lost any interest in trying. In the wider empire it did not even try. It was becoming too obvious that religious pluralism was an absolutely necessary foundation for imperial growth and stability: Hindus in India, Catholics in Quebec or Malta were simply the facts of life. England would need in consequence to relate to Rome itself in a new and unconfrontatory manner, displeasing as this might be to many. To start with this could seem just a matter of coping with marginal areas diplomatically, but as regions of Catholic dominance within the dominions of the King of England multiplied, and the ensuring of their loyalty became a matter of central imperial policy, and as Catholics were seen so to hold together that you could hardly illtreat them in one place without repercussions elsewhere, it became necessary in the course of the nineteenth century for the England-Rome relationship to alter quite integrally. Indeed, the issue of church-state relations within the British Empire became once more a matter of how Westminster related to Rome in a mutually profitable manner, still more than how it related to Lambeth. Lambeth did not matter equally just because it could be counted upon so much more easily. It was separated from the state by no uncertain distance. Rome could not so obviously be counted on, but could be needed all the more. Yet, in due course England and Rome came each to see that it could again actually rely on the other, and that in policy they had much in common, however much each also needed to maintain between themselves an adequate distance.

It is true that upon the British side an almost paranoid distrust of Catholicism remained powerful throughout the Victorian age. As late as 1874, when the Marquis of Ripon, one of Gladstone's closest colleagues in the leadership of the Liberal Party, became a Catholic, *The Times* declared in a leading article that 'a statesman who becomes a convert to Roman Catholicism forfeits at once the confidence of the English people. Such a step involves a complete abandonment of any claim to political or even social influence in the nation at large and can only be regarded as betraying an irreparable weakness of character' (5 September 1874). Yet, in point of fact Ripon was to be an influential member of many Liberal cabinets after that, as well as Viceroy of India.

If Catholicism could no longer be ignored or insulted lest it make the whole system unworkable, then it had, rather, to be deftly contained and this proved not too hard to manage once there was the will to do so. Ireland provided the principal prototype for the new relationship between Britain and Catholicism and a case closer to, and more influential upon, the centre of the imperial system than Quebec or Malta. In Malta the Catholic Church remained essentially established and no Anglican bishop could be allowed there. The appointment of its Catholic bishop might matter to the British government at least as much as that of the Archbishop of York. Could the model of a controlled Catholic establishment be further extended, even to Ireland? The Maynooth Grant, whereby the British government actually contributed to the training of Irish Catholic priests, was a first step which might have led to a far more established church—even, conceivably, to the 'concurrent' establishment in Ireland of two churches, Catholic and Protestant. Similarly it was proposed by some that Catholic Emancipation in England should go with the requirement that the government must approve the appointment of Catholic bishops. Fortunately these lines were not followed up. There was not the will to do so on either side. Each recognised the value, even the moral necessity, of a greater measure of distance.

Nevertheless the more the new relationship developed, the more useful it became to both sides. Indeed the Catholic Church proved by far the most reliable of imperial churches—more so, really, even than the Anglican. Anglicans felt enough at home to be at times tiresome critics and the Church of England was not good at suppressing its more turbulent clerics—a C. F. Andrews or an Arthur Shearly Cripps. The Church of Rome could keep its priests on a far firmer rein. Few colonial governors ever needed to lose a night's sleep over any Catholic missionary: they became the most reliable pillars for the *Pax Britannica*. The very fact that few were actually British gave them an extra note of caution but it was chiefly that Catholic missionaries—French, Dutch, Italian or Irish—were Tories at heart, recruited from areas of conservative social sympathies, with very few exceptions. As a consequence, the British imperial system—not suddenly and not with any very explicit statement of policy, but increasingly and profoundly—came to welcome and even encourage the Catholic missionary system as a valuable and almost universal adjunct of empire.

Take Uganda in the early 1890s, a time when the relationship was still far from fully developed. When French Catholic White Fathers and English Church Missionary Society men clashed, their adherents turned to civil war and the Catholic Cathedral at Rubaga went up in flames as the Protestants, assisted by Captain Lugard, won the battle of Mengo, it was already exceedingly embarrassing from a British imperial point of view. The empire could only be built upon a certain ecclesiastical impartiality and it could not afford to alienate the omnipresent Catholic missionary, or to face accusations in the House of Lords from the Duke of Norfolk of anti-Catholic discrimination.

It was even more embarrassing to seem to give the government of France an excuse for interfering in a British sphere of interest by posing as the protector of Catholic interests. The odd reality of this affair was that Britain still appeared as very much a Protestant power to most British, French and African eyes alike, but was in reality striving quite hard not to be (for much of the affair Ripon was actually Colonial Secretary!). It is interesting that at least one English Catholic bishop, Patterson, the titular bishop of Emmaus, supported Lugard and concluded 'it is such folly for us not to have a duly accredited agent at Rome to give the Pope *authentic* accounts of things all over the British Empire' (Margery Perham, *Lugard, the Years of Adventure*, 1956, p. 375).

Lugard and his successors in fact went out of their way to establish an equitable settlement. The tendency of both missionaries and native Christians in Uganda had been to interpret British rule in terms of Protestant ascendancy. This was indeed part of a wider pattern. Anglican ecclesiastics tended to insinuate some sort of quasi-establishment of the Church of England in British colonies. In ceremonial terms—and a little more too—they frequently got their way. Nevertheless it was crucial to the larger imperial purpose to demonstrate that this was not really the case, and by and large it succeeded. In point of fact British Catholics were already by 1890 the empire's chosen representatives in lots of places other than Uganda. Sir James Marshall had been a key figure upon the west African coast until his death in 1889. In the Malay Colonial Service there were a whole bunch of men drawn from the best Old Catholic families. In Rhodesia Mother Patrick and her Dominican Sisters were at just the same time as the Ugandan civil war acclaimed heroines of the pioneer column. An overt anti-Catholicism might still be tolerated in Lewes in 1890. On the colonial frontier it just would not work. If Arthur Grimble's *Pattern of Islands* represents the later imperial mood as well as anything, the colonial official's beloved foil, almost *alter ego*, was here the French Catholic missionary, Fr Choblet.

Looked at from the other end, that of Rome, the position appeared not so dissimilar. The decisive point in the process of change is to be located around 1870. The collapse of the Papal States and the founding of new missionary societies, the disestablishment of the Church of Ireland, all opened the path to a great shift, both a broadening and a deepening, in the Romano-British relationship. Thus the Mill Hill Fathers, England's national missionary society, founded in 1867, would be particularly loyal servants of the empire as well as the church. Rome and its missionary societies were habituated to expect some discrimination from a Protestant power but were relieved to find it less and less (unlike the experience of Protestant missionaries in Portuguese or Belgian Africa). In practice, the more the great nineteenth-century Catholic missionary movement got under way, the more it needed a benevolent British Empire, and the more it found in most places what it needed. It found tolerance, stability, order, respect for property, freedom to evangelise, even grants for its schools, and a great willingness to let an international church operate internationally. The Portuguese state or the Belgian state might appear very Catholic, but their jealous nationalisms could prove extremely awkward for the church. One would insist upon the appointment of only Portuguese bishops, the other of Belgians. The British state, on the contrary, was perfectly willing to have within its frontiers French, German, Italian, Dutch bishops. It is clear enough why, by the 1880s, Leo XIII was extremely anxious to enter into formal diplomatic relations with Great Britain.

Not only ecclesiastically but politically Westminster and the Vatican shared common interests. The Irish example remains the most obviously instructive. It was, I think, often felt in Ireland that the British Government must be constantly intriguing in Rome to ensure that the Pope did not support Irish Nationalism. And the Pope did not. But on the whole this was not, it seems, because of British pressure so much as because that was the way Rome itself wanted to be. It is perfectly true that nationalism had a lot to do with making the Irish such devout Catholics yet, paradoxically, what mattered to the Catholic Church was rather their convenient British status, and mastery of the English language. An Ireland within the British Empire was a great deal more useful to Rome than an Ireland without. Irish migration gave a new look of healthy young growth to world Catholicism in the latter half of the nineteenth century and the empire did much to make it easy. But it is also true that the modern Irish missionary movement was slow in developing. At least until the 1920s Irish missionaries mattered a good deal less in Asia or Africa than French, Belgian, Dutch or German ones. Rome needed to make use of them all, and was disinclined to spare much sympathy for the nationalist quirks of any one group. Moreover, how could the papacy really support nationalism in Ireland when it so much misliked nationalism in Italy? The Pope had not the slightest objection to the Emperor of Austria ruling Croatia or Slovakia. How could he object to English rule in Ireland? Papal policy was both consistent and essentially Tory and—at least from a window in Rome—Hapsburg rule over the Balkans, British rule over India, Nigeria or Ireland, could seem politically proper and ecclesiastically useful.

By the early twentieth century a basic harmony of interest was pretty clearly recognised upon both sides. Edward VII's visit to Pope Leo in 1903 was an imaginative personal gesture, the first encounter between an English monarch and a pope since the Reformation. At the time it still seemed to the politicians a somewhat rash gesture yet it was in its way programmatic for the coming century. All the same, for the time being a considerable distance was still deliberately maintained, a distance derived from both theology and history and sustained by much emotional sentiment, particularly on the British side and the home front. The heat produced by the Eucharistic Congress in London in 1908 and the cancellation of its public procession through the streets of Westminster is a good example. The publicly equivocal nature of the relationship between church and state could hardly be better illustrated. Permission for a public procession had been granted well in advance—by the Commissioner of the Metropolitan Police, Sir Edward Henry, himself an Irish Catholic. At the very last moment Protestant objections were sufficient to upset the king and prime minister: 'There is a good deal of quite respectable Protestant sentiment', Asquith wrote to Lord Crewe, 'Which is offended by this gang of foreign cardinals taking advantage of our hospitality to parade their idolatries through the streets of London' (Roy Jenkins, *Asquith*, 1978, p. 191), and poor old Lord Ripon, very near to death, was pushed into persuading Cardinal Bourne to call it off. Clearly at this point neither public sentiment nor the personal outlook of the premier had caught up with political reality: if London was the capital of a world-wide empire, in which the Catholic Church was a power of major importance, a religious procession through a few side streets should hardly have merited such a reaction. It was one of the ambiguities of the relationship that, upon the British side, there was a long-surviving inability quite to admit either its reality or its implications.

Until at least the First World War, the sense of being a Protestant nation remained a powerful container on the British government's freedom of initiative. At the leadership level Asquith, Balfour, the Chamberlains or Anthony Eden had, none of them, the slightest personal attraction for, or understanding of, Roman religion. Quite the opposite. Well into the 1930s the pundits of the Foreign Office had to put a lot of hidden pressure on Neville Chamberlain, when visiting Rome, to call upon the Pope. The maintenance of distance, however, was being quietly eroded by two principal factors: a bridging element and the pressure of new circumstances.

Let us consider the bridging element first. Protestant as the British establishment undoubtedly was, it had near its heart a small but by no means insignificant catholic minority; the upper-class recusant families to which were joined a select band of nineteenth-century aristocratic converts. You could not ignore the Duke of Norfolk, particularly the 15th Duke, and his relatives and friends. They possessed all the proper qualities of the British establishment. They were utterly reliable as senior citizens of the empire. In such circles being a Catholic, for instance, in no way meant being over-sympathetic to Irish home rule. If they could be trusted, they could not be ignored. They owned too many English acres for that. And yet, they were also a remarkably loyal group of Roman Catholics: educated at the Oratory, Stonyhurst or Downside, devout, respectful to the bishops, very willing indeed to speak out for Catholic interests—schools at home, the freedom of missionaries abroad—wherever this seemed needed.

A few brief biographies illustrate our bridge adequately enough. The first is that of Lord Edmund FitzAlan-Howard, brother of the 15th Duke of Norfolk. Two of his sisters were nuns—one a Carmelite, the other a sister of charity—and he was hardly less devout than they. He was MP for Chichester 1894-1921 and Conservative Chief Whip for the later years. He was Lord Lieutenant of Ireland 1921-2 being created Viscount FitzAlan at the same time. He was the first Catholic to preside in Dublin Castle and the last Englishman to do so. He became President of the Catholic Union in 1923 and was the personal friend and consultant of Cardinals from Vaughan to Hinsley, but he was also a close friend of George V and lived next door to Windsor Castle in Cumberland Lodge in the Great Park. The second is James Hope, from 1932 Lord Rankeillour, Lord Edmund's nephew. Like his uncle he was at the Oratory School. When his other uncle, the Duke of Norfolk, was Postmaster-General in Salisbury's cabinet, Hope was his secretary. He was Deputy Speaker of the House of Commons through most of the 1920s and chairman of committees. His wife was President of the Catholic Women's League. Undoubtedly there were few people of this weight but the list could be extended even to include a few Irishmen like Sir Nicholas O'Conor and Count John de Salis who was the British Minister to the Holy See from 1916 to 1922—it was, doubtless, convenient to have a Catholic Irishman from County Limerick (if educated at Eton) to represent Britain in Rome in the very awkward years after the Easter Rising.

Sir Nicholas, an O'Conor from County Roscommon and cousin of the O'Conor Don, was a major diplomat with formidable experience in Peking, St Petersburg and Constantinople where he died as British ambassador in 1908. The Duke of Norfolk's niece was O'Conor's wife, James Hope was a nephew, Lord FitzAlan a younger brother. It is indeed hard to doubt that the 15th Duke in his fifty years and more in that role had more to do than anyone else in the development we are considering.

By far the most important (and wealthy) layman in the half century between the 1860s and the First World War during which the relationship between the Catholic church and the British state was so decisively, if subtly, transformed, the Duke was also one of the most devout. Builder of the cathedral-like churches at Norwich and Arundel and President of the Catholic Union, he had been Queen Victoria's special envoy to Pope Leo in 1887, the year of the Golden Jubilee. He was a cabinet minister through much of the 1890s, and he ordered the coronations of Edward VII and George V with great imagination, reviving many ancient customs. He was in fact a sort of quiet incarnation of the emerging *entente cordiale* between church and state, and the final comment of the *Dictionary of National Biography* after his death is significant: 'He reminded his friends of Sir Thomas More; and the parallel is not without interest since the Duke was the first Catholic layman, since the death of More, who had played a great and honourable part in English public life'. Remarkably much the same might be said of FitzAlan. Around them, their relatives and friends were finding it once more both possible and profitable to be 'the King's good servants, but God's first'.

Such people were totally at home within the inner circle of British power but equally at home within Catholicism. It is unlikely that they ever felt the slightest sense of a conflict of loyalties and their existence ensured that, whenever necessary, the two hierarchies—the Catholic ecclesiastical and the British political—understood one another. They were also clearly available as trouble-shooters when and where the British Empire was faced with problems of a specially Catholic dimension. It was a small group but just sufficient: without its unobtrusive mediating role past suspicions upon either side would have persisted far more than they did and could even have been magnified in the tensions engendered both by colonial rule and by European totalitarian politics.

The British Legation to the Holy See was first established on a temporary basis at the start of the war, in 1914, the Apostolic Delegation in London in 1938, despite, in each case, a few protests. It is noteworthy that in both cases—Sir Henry Howard and the Count de Salis on the one hand, Archbishop Godfrey on the other—British Catholics were the first appointees, if subsequently succeeded by Protestants upon the one hand, non-British on the other. The initial bridge function is clear. The Legation in Rome represents a British initiative, the Delegation in London a Roman. The establishment of the first indicates the moment at which Whitehall decided that the Vatican was too important to be cold-shouldered on account of either the Quirinale or the Protestant conscience. The presence in Rome of Cardinal Gasquet was simply not good enough when it came to a defence of imperial interests. The pressures of war-time diplomacy and an increasingly disturbed Ireland forced the pace as the needs of the nineteenth-century empire, grave as they were, had never quite managed to do. It was indeed, in terms of British imperial need, late in coming. The second indicates the moment at which the Vatican decided that Britain was just too important to be left in the hands of the Archbishop of Westminster—too frigid in the case of Bourne, too impulsive in the case of Hinsley.

If the inherited sentiments of mutual distrust were steadily declining in these years, the need for a tacit alliance, for a recognition of shared values, and a mechanism for consultation and the resolving of minor practical differences between the world's largest empire and largest church was equally steadily increasing. Gone were the days when the papacy's political influence in Europe or elsewhere could be dismissed, and the advance of Fascism and—still more—Nazism meant that both Britain and the papacy were, in an increasingly worrying world, wanting all the support they could find from the more or less like-minded. Of course, differences of attitude remained: Britain had a somewhat greater theoretical interest in democracy than had Rome—but not so much greater. Too much democracy abroad could after all only be disastrous for the future of the empire. Britain's social policy was in fair harmony with that of the social encyclicals.

The British government in truth was not more interested in the immediate flourishing of parliamentary democracy in Spain than it could be in India. It *was* worried about the spread of communism or about anything which could push a victorious Franco into full alliance with Hitler. And while the Vatican's fear of communism might be a little greater than Whitehall's, its position was very little different. The Falange for both was distasteful but not unbearable. And the more Europe fell victim to either Nazism or communism, the more clearly the policy makers of the Vatican and Whitehall saw how closely together they needed to stand, while still not appearing to do so too obviously. Britain immensely appreciated the increasingly firm anti-Nazi stance of Pius XI, and was extremely relieved that Cardinal Pacelli succeeded him, though disappointed that he proved as Pius XII to be far less outspoken than his predecessor. In particular, up to June 1940, they shared a policy objective absolutely crucial to both and which each believed the other could help with—keeping Italy from joining the war on Hitler's side. But over a much wider field the pressures of the Second World War greatly helped to reveal to both empire and church, as never before, how much they had in common. The character of Cardinal Hinsley—as also the character of d'Arcy Osborne, British Minister to the

Holy See 1940-44—contributed not a little to that experience of mutual rediscovery, even if it did not quite survive those very special years.

It might seem odd—and offensive to the Protestant conscience— that the bright young Under-Secretary at the Foreign Office, R. A. Butler, could refer in the House of Commons itself to Pius XI as 'the Holy Father', but it represented well enough the sense of respect, partnership and mutual understanding which had now been reached.

The relationship I have endeavoured to sketch remained characteristically British rather than Roman. The chosen Roman approaches to church-state relations in the first half of the twentieth century were the formal concordat, the movement of *Catholic Action* and, in places, the church-orientated political party. In all these, at least until the Second World War, the clergy were the primary operators. Not one of these models enters seriously into our relationship which remains, furthermore, unusually open to lay initiative. There was a very strong sense of Catholic fellowship within the empire, the sense that Catholics could not be ill-treated in one place without repercussions elsewhere, but this was coupled with a sense of what constituted a legitimate Catholic interest and what did not. Breaking up the empire or altering its structure of government was not. Home Rule was not. Even challenging the aura of Anglican ascendency was not (was not the Duke of Norfolk's primary task as Earl Marshal the ordering of the greatest of all Anglican ceremonies, the coronation of the monarch—oath to maintain the Protestant religion and all?). But religious and educational freedom everywhere was. Equality before the law and the opportunity of individual advancement was. So was public opposition to anti-religious forces.

English Catholicism was, above all, committed to constitutionality, to freedom, even—in an untheoretical, undemagogic way—to respect for parliamentary democracy. It was itself, effectively, a free church and it was a suspicion that the ultramontane spirit was both unfree and unEnglish which made English upper-class Catholics empathise a great deal more with Newman than with Manning. Yet Manning's own ultramontanism, unlike that of most of his contemporaries in Rome or elsewhere, was one which went with full support for working-class democracy; indeed his criticism of the English Catholic tradition was partly that it was too aristocratic and not democratic enough. Belloc, in his anti-democratic, anti-parliamentary moods, reflected a profound note of French Catholicism—to which he partly belonged and much admired —but far less of English. (Only in the inter-war period did the English Catholic intelligensia—partly under Belloc's influence—temporarily flirt with fascism to an unpleasant yet still rather superficial extent.) Even if

Acton was in many ways the *enfant terrible,* the odd man out of late Victorian English Catholicism, he did still—in his intellectual preoccupation with the relationship between freedom and organised religion—represent his community fairly enough. English Catholics from Manning to Norfolk might disagree with Gladstone's judgement upon the political reliability of Catholics from the viewpoint of a liberal state, but they largely accepted his view of the nature of that state and the proper relationship of the church to it. In this they differed very considerably from contemporary Catholics upon the continent. Ludicrously remote from the reality of English Catholicism as they might seem, Gladstone's strictures in his *Expostulation* on the reliability of the civil allegiance of Catholics made rather more sense in relation to the *Syllabus of Errors* and the formal political poise of the papacy of Pius IX. The value of English Catholics lay—to the church as much as to the state—in the sincerity of their 'liberalism', their pragmatic repudiation of the *Syllabus of Errors* and all its ways (Tories though they probably were by 1900 in party political terms).

The strength of the Catholic position was, paradoxically, that its justification lay in terms of the British rather than the Roman tradition. Yet it was still, it could be claimed, a Catholic tradition, and not wholly an untheological one—of the English Cisalpine variety. Newman had, after all, commented publicly upon the first Vatican Council in the form of *A Letter to the Duke of Norfolk,* 'Hereditary Earl Marshal of England etc, etc'. He had written (replying to Mr Gladstone explicitly, but implicitly almost as much to Cardinal Manning) at the Duke's urging on the question 'Can Catholics be trustworthy subjects of the State?' and he claimed the Duke on his opening page, accurately enough, as 'the special representative and the fitting sample of a laity, as zealous for the Catholic Religion as it is patriotic'. It was the year, let us recall, of Lord Ripon's conversion. Remember that the Duke at this time was a young man in his mid-twenties who had been, ten years earlier—like his brother, Lord FitzAlan—a pupil at Newman's Oratory School in Birmingham. Remember too that the Duke remained a devoted disciple and it was his appeal—and Lord Ripon's—five years later which would result in Pope Leo making Newman a Cardinal. In an earlier paper published in the *Rambler,* much misliked by ultramontanes, Newman had written 'On Consulting the Faithful in matters of Doctrine'. How much more, one might say, in matters of politics and church-state relations. In these writings Newman was providing something of a theological foundation for the British Catholic relationship and the role of the English Catholic elite within it which was in point of fact about to develop. Indeed, those famous, much quoted lines in the *Letter* on conscience might well be regarded as constituting the very charter of the relationship's viability: 'If I am obliged to bring religion into after-dinner toasts (which indeed does not seem quite the thing), I shall drink—to the Pope, if you please—still, to conscience first, and to the Pope afterwards'.

It was the role which the English Catholic upper class had long aspired to—*that* was indeed much of what Cisalpinism was about. It was a role which could not possibly be filled if Catholics were to be excluded from the national universities as Manning wished them to be. Newman's attempt to establish a house at Oxford pointed to a necessary aspect of a new political relationship. Manning forbade it. He died and his policies were reversed. Before the nineteenth century was over the Duke of Norfolk was actually founding St Edmund's House, a centre of Catholic clerical study at Cambridge. In this again he was the pupil of Newman. Newman, it has been remarked, 'remained an isolated figure, away from the mainstream of ecclesiastical business' (Edward Norman, *Roman Catholicism in England*, 1986, p. 96). That is, of course, very true and yet part of our thesis is that his relationship with the young Duke of Norfolk, even his innate Toryism, made him eventually extremely influential in political and educational terms. If theologically and clergy-wise, ultramontanism triumphed in the late Victorian English Catholic Church, politically and lay-wise Cisalpinism was far more effectively successful than has been recognised. For this both Newman and the Duke of Norfolk have considerable responsibility.

Paradoxically, as we have already seen, this success proved extremely useful to Rome and the ultramontane cause generally in a way that the success of a more ultramontane policy could not have been. In theory Rome would for long continue to prefer other models. In practice it would soon be finding this the most reliably suited to its needs, but it would not be until after the Second World War that it became (if with much less of an aristocratic note) something nearer the norm than the anomaly.

If Newman, who seems so marginal to the polity of English Catholicism, turns out then to be on the contrary central enough to the developing shape of its relationship to the political establishment, Manning—his ecclesiastical opposite—who in life undoubtedly dominated church-state relations, might seem in retrospect to have had his legacy too largely discarded. Cardinal Manning was by far the greatest English churchman of the Victorian era, just as Newman was its greatest theologian. One detects in him a note of emphatic rejection of any collusion with the established *status quo*, either social or religious, to which, far more than Newman, he had nevertheless belonged by class and disposition. For him conversion to Rome went with a conversion away from the wider viewpoint of the British ruling class. He was of course in no way disloyal to the state, and remained a more active participant in the formulation of its high policy than any other Archbishop of Westminster, but he was, and very especially in later life, a thorough-going social radical. He supported the causes of Irish nationalism. He supported London's striking dockers. He wanted to keep Catholics away from the social privileges of Oxford. There was in Manning—who called himself 'a Mosaic Radical'—a dimension of liberation theology, no less, wholly absent from Newman as from by far the greater part of nineteenth-century Catholicism. Cardinals Vaughan and Bourne, who followed him at Westminster, were his faithful enough heirs ecclesiastically, but politically they were miles away. In 1926 when Archbishop Davidson was proposing a compromise over the General Strike to conservative dismay, Cardinal Bourne was declaring the Strike a mortal sin, to conservative delight. Apart from a touch of populism in Hinsley, there would be little further trace of Manning's political radicalism in clerical Catholicism until the empire had ceased to exist, and not much among the laity either.

If Manning's political influence upon Gladstone could be considerable, it was hardly less with Leo XIII. Unlike Manning Leo was not a democrat and there is a vast difference in spirit between the caution of *Rerum Novarum* and Manning's evident devotion to the struggle of the poor. Nevertheless in the encyclicals of the 1880s and 1890s Leo had moved very far from his predecessor's approach in the *Syllabus of Errors* and was effectively formulating the basis for a new relationship between the church and the modern state. He was undoubtedly influenced by Manning in this at several points and in fact this provided the theoretical undergirding upon the Roman side for the more pragmatic relationship we have been considering. Manning's liberationism was held in check all the same by an effective sense of practical politics, of what we may fairly call the church's main chance. Thus it was clear to him—however much he wanted justice for Ireland—that it would in no way serve the church's interests if all Irish MPs were to be removed from Westminster to Dublin. As he shrewdly wrote to Leo XIII in 1885, citing Michael Davitt, 'from the point of view of the head of the Catholic Church, the transference of forty or fifty Catholic members from the highest Protestant assembly of the world . . . cannot be a victory for the cause of the Catholic Church' (17 February 1885, Shane Leslie, *Henry Edward Manning*, 1921, pp. 402-3).

If Manning more than anyone else was responsible for the new church-state relationship, and aware of its intrinsic possibilities, it is sad that the challenging freedom he brought to it was so largely lost. Yet his liberationist radicalism—if carried on by colonial bishops in comparable circumstances—could certainly have imperilled it. (The stance of Archbishop Mannix of Melbourne over many decades represents all that Britain was most anxious to avoid in official Catholicism, but it could easily have been more widely represented.) The Catholic Church was so appropriate a partner for the British Empire just because, while bowing respectfully if at times a little awkwardly to the constitutional and democratic model of political life, its preferences remained so consistently for the Tory not the liberal—and still less the radical—mode. If it had been domesticated by the empire a little too easily, it was because that is just what the Church of the time above all preferred.

It may be enlightening also to ask what was the effect of the establishment of the Church of England upon the relationship we have been sketching. Clearly in the earlier stages they were seen to be in a necessary rivalry. Any advance of Rome within the royal dominions was seen as something of an affront to the established church; the reality of the advance could not be prevented but at least it might be rejected symbolically as in the *Ecclesiastical Titles Act* of 1851. At the English provincial level a stress upon the incompatibility of rival claims might last deep into the twentieth century, but at a national, political and colonial level it was being replaced by increasing elements, not merely of co-existence, but of a covert alliance. Catholics disputed the principle of establishment less than Free Churchmen and in fact the Catholic Church actually benefited from its existence. Catholic schools would never have begun to be subsidised by the Education Act of 1902 were Church of England schools not needing subsidy too. The whole structure of Anglicanism from Archbishop to curate prepared Englishmen, high church, low church or agnostic, for an essentially similar structure in Catholicism. The British state was in some way committed to Christianity and bound at least to be respectful of its representatives, as France was not, and this in practice provided a useful starting point for Catholic relations with government at least as much as Methodist or Congregationalist. Cardinal Bourne declared that he had no difficulty in obtaining a meeting with any cabinet minister when he wanted it and by at least the time of Lang and Hinsley a quite considerable *entente* had been established enabling them to undertake a measure of joint action when they so wished. The benefits of establishment were in fact washing off on the Catholic Church to a moderate but convenient extent, so far as it desired it. The benefits without the disadvantages. Anglican bishops enjoyed their presence in the House of Lords and at times made speeches of importance, but it had its awkward side. If they supported the government or the majority line, they could seem too domesticated; if they did not, they could be exposed to fairly uncomfortable counter charges. The Catholic bishops enjoyed the freedom of being outside the system while having enough Catholic peers, and generally a few Commons too, absolutely ready to express their views when required—and to field the resultant brickbats as well. Similarly it is noticeable that they left lay people as editors of the principal Catholic papers—even those owned by the Church. Very few members of the Catholic clerical leadership belonged socially, as its lay leadership did, to the British establishment and this helped maintain a sense of distance prior to the age of Basil Hume. Perhaps Archbishop David Mathew was the only priest of importance to do so and his seven-year tenure of the Apostolic Delegation to British East and West Africa after the Second World War in fact marked a high point at the imperial level in the smooth running of the church-state relationship. For Anglicans their involvement was far greater than their power, and that can be dangerous. For Catholics, their power at least seemed rather more considerable than their involvement, and that should be seen as constituting a position of strength.

Finally, if, of course, there always remained between empire and church a certain distance in sympathy, an ability on the home front to be even a little niggling at times, a determination to keep the concordat secret (almost from themselves), this too was highly beneficial to both sides. Church and state may benefit in various ways from assisting each other, but they seldom benefit from appearing to do so. The maintenance of distance is at least as important as the ability to co-operate. The relationship between the British Empire and the Roman Catholic Church, as it grew to fullness in the former's final period of ascendancy between the two world wars, contained the realities of a concordat without the awkward encumbrance of juridical detail and theoretical loss of freedom in the formal variety. In this it was, after all, very characteristic of the British Constitution.

Chapter Four

What Matters To Us Now

George Bell was Bishop of Chichester from 1929 to 1958. He had been Randall Davidson's chaplain for ten years and then his biographer. In both roles he had seen the struggle of a profoundly erastian archbishop endeavouring most conscientiously to respond to the ceaseless problems of the world, and especially the political world, around him. Very occasionally, and most notably in regard to the General Strike, Davidson was persuaded of the need to act and speak publicly in a truly independent way. Mostly he did not. Of his eminently sane condemnation in 1918 of the anti-German mania incited by Lloyd George, at that time Prime Minister, Bell comments 'It was a misfortune that the Archbishop, though entertaining these opinions, did not proclaim them to the world' (Bell, 1935, p. 842).

It is there that an erastian church crosses the Rubicon. Bell was deeply Anglican of a quite traditional kind and by temperament no radical but he had an exceptionally clear mind and, having long pondered the example of Davidson, he became resolved not to follow it. He would, on the contrary, proclaim his opinions to the world in the course of the Second World War, however embarrassing such opinions frequently were to the government. Davidson did so occasionally and hesitantly. Bell was prepared to do so regularly and without a sense that he needed to excuse himself. He remembered the lamentable First World War jingoism of the then Bishop of London, Winnington-Ingram, and he remembered the far more Christian silences of Archbishop Davidson. This time, if he could help it, the church would not sink to being no more than 'the State's spiritual auxiliary'. At the very start of the war in November 1939 he wrote an article in the *Fortnightly Review* entitled 'The Church's Function in War Time' to which he remained extraordinarily faithful. 'When all the resources of the State are concentrated, for example, on winning a war, the Church is not part of these resources . . . It possesses an authority independent of the State . . . It is not the State's spiritual auxiliary with exactly the same ends as the State'.

His first battle was over the internment of thousands of Germans and Italians without discrimination, though many of them were refugees, as 'enemy aliens' in rather harsh conditions. His second was to try and persuade the government to encourage the German opposition, including his friend Bonhoeffer, to stage a revolution by expressing willingness to negotiate with a non-Nazi government. It refused to do so. His third was to urge the government to take what steps it could to save European Jewry from extermination. It was not interested in trying. His fourth, and that in which he came into most open conflict with government policy, was his attack upon the obliteration bombing of German towns. In these years George Bell became the first Anglican bishop to speak out, not on a special occasion, but regularly, in a manner that was quite out of line with the mind of government. If Davidson had moved distinctly beyond his predecessors towards an essential autonomy of approach to matters of public importance, Bell had moved way beyond Davidson.

He was much helped in this, I believe, by his chairmanship for some years of *Life and Work*, the international ecumenical movement, during the 1930s. He was in consequence no longer just bishop of Chichester appointed by the king but had the independence of a major position in the world church. The erastian mind does not easily aggregate with significant international responsibilities. In this Bell developed rather differently from his still more distinguished contemporary, William Temple. While Temple attended, and indeed chaired, many important ecumenical gatherings, they seem more marginal to his consciousness. He remained, I would judge, at heart, very much more of an erastian than did Bell, and by temperament a monist. As a young man he had indeed led the Anglican 'Life and Liberty' movement with Dick Sheppard. 'We demand liberty for the Church of England' he had cried at a famous meeting in 1917. That suggests a note of dualism which was appropriate to the moment but it led to relatively little 'liberty' at the time and it was not a note characteristic of his genius.

The element of separation, conflict, *angst*, in human living seemed almost to pass him by. If perhaps he failed to be the 'prophet' he was often hailed to be, it was most of all because he lacked Bell's ability to recognise the inevitability of disagreement, even of evil, and the need to speak sharply across it, to be willing on occasion to separate himself, even from the British government, to be in an obstinate minority rather than a consensus voice. But if Temple (like his successor at Canterbury, Geoffrey Fisher) was among the last and greatest Anglican representatives of the old establishment mind of a relatively full sort, Bell was one of the first Anglicans in high position to reclaim the role of prophecy and to recognise the need for a dualist distancing of church from state. Despite his background he was caught up (and that can be dangerous too) in the moral primacy of speaking the whole truth at the present moment, whether Caesar likes it or not. For non-erastians he made the surviving elements of establishment almost desirable. In doing so, he was in point of fact—perhaps without quite seeing it himself—altering the goal posts. In traditional terms he was ceasing to be a good Anglican and many good Anglicans deeply resented his interventions. But he would be, in consequence, a more appropriate model than Temple for the Anglican Communion of the future.

A few decades earlier than this, the English Free Churches had moved rather rapidly, if briefly, in a different direction, and this too may have some lessons for us. As Nonconformists multiplied through the nineteenth century their determination both to alter their own legally underprivileged position and otherwise to enter political life for the sake of realising their social ideals had steadily increased, escaping from the rather apolitical vacuum in which they had been forced to exist ever since the age of Cromwell. It was the extension of the franchise in 1867 and, again, in 1884 to include men of the lower middle classes and upper working class which really made of them a potentially powerful political force. The great number of divisions within Nonconformity and the relatively leaderless character of free churches in comparison with episcopal churches, made it difficult, nevertheless, for nonconformists to mobilise themselves in such a way as to have an impact upon national government. Nonconformist ecclesiology tends to diffuse the church-state relationship. To some extent they countered this through the development of a National Council of the Free Churches, but a semi-ecumenical body of this sort had a limited effectiveness. It is hardly surprising that the Nonconformist voice came to be mediated above all through non-ecclesiastical organisations, first of all the Liberation Society, in regard to the campaign for disestablishment, but then, and very much more, through the Liberal Party.

The relationship between Liberals and Nonconformists was always a somewhat one-sided one. If a large proportion of the core of Liberal support was undoubtedly Nonconformist, few of the party's leaders were. While the Liberal Party was always anxious not to upset Nonconformist susceptibilities, if it could help it, it seldom showed any great determination to push through the Nonconformist agenda. That is perhaps hardly surprising when one thinks what a moralistic ragbag that agenda largely was. Indignation over single issues, the rise and fall of particular 'crusades' erupting from the latest enthusiasm of the Nonconformist conscience, were not the stuff of effective politics. The greatest and most long-lasting of these crusades was over education, the struggle to repeal Balfour's Education Act of 1902 which had granted rate aid to Church of England and, even worse, Roman Catholic schools. Yet, despite the efforts of several well-meaning Presidents of the Board of Education, nothing was ever achieved educationally. What was achieved was a brief but disastrous politicisation of Nonconformity to provide a sort of standing army for the Liberal government. Some of the ablest of Nonconformist ministers, like the Baptist John Clifford and the Congregationalist Sylvester Horne, remained for years extraordinarily caught up in this 'Holy Alliance' with the Liberal Party machine. Horne became a Member of Parliament at the same time as being chairman of the Congregational Union. Clifford spoke again and again at election times on the same platform as Lloyd George. In 1909 a Congregationalist minister published anonymously a book entitled *Nonconformity and Politics* in which he suggested that a visitor would hardly be able to distinguish a typical Free Church Council public meeting from one of the Liberal Party. Its publication signalled the beginnings of disillusionment.

In the 'Holy alliance', one may suggest, a rather simplistic attempt to relate the church effectively to the modern political world in a non-establishment way damaged the church while achieving next to nothing politically. The point of recalling this here is to remind ourselves that there is more than one way to kill a cat, more than one way in which a church, rightly concerned with the political, can nevertheless lose its critical distance through being drawn—even against the whole ethos of its own tradition—too closely within the political structure. The latter might do it one way with the Church of England, another way with Nonconformity, a third way with Catholicism. Each thought it gained by establishment, implicit concordat or holy alliance. And, of course, in some ways it did. Yet each could quite easily be in danger of losing more than it gained.

In this case it was, furthermore, Nonconformity which pressed its services upon the Liberal Party rather than the other way round. And the Liberal Party, even the Liberal Government, was not the state. Indeed it was precisely the inability of the Liberal Government to control the enduring structures of the establishment, in this case especially the House of Lords, which most enraged Free Churchmen. Paradoxically an anti-establishment moral indignation, derived from a long dualist tradition, fuelled this brief expression of monism. One might hypothesize that if a Liberal government, led by Lloyd George, had lasted in peacetime, the 'Holy Alliance' could have hardened into a lasting new form of monism. However, this would seem too deeply repugnant to

Nonconformist traditions to be probable. While temporarily of some use to the Liberal Party, it quickly damaged and divided Nonconformity, which began to react against it quite fast. Dualists are not easily converted into monists, though it may be that monists are still less easily turned into dualists.

That may be true. Nevertheless, the greatest mistake in analysis would be to contrast dualist and monist too sharply. The integration of church and state is so very much a matter of degree. In principle there are three alternative models. Religion can be wholly integrated with society in such a way that it might be said, for instance, in traditional Africa that to be a Kikuyu was itself a religion. The character of Christianity makes it almost impossible for this ever to be quite the case, unlike the character of Islam, but in practice medieval society and, in theory, the doctrine of Justinian or Hooker went as far as could be in this direction. Religion may also be wholly differentiated from secular life in dualist terms. However, a fully sectarian programme of withdrawal from 'the world' can easily land one back pretty close to our first model. Life among the Closed Brethren or the Mormons or in a large contemplative monastery or any other group which has more or less segregated its members in terms of employment, recreation, and even geographically becomes in practice rather like the life of a tribe. Any practical distinction between church and society effectively disappears. Such a religiously constructed mini-society inevitably behaves more and more like a monist state. Both of these ultimately totalitarian models exclude the possibility of dualism, of living in two kinds of society at the same time, each of which can claim an authority not obtained from the other. It is this which characterises our third model, that of a church differentiated from society by its faith, its rituals, its sense of spiritual communion, but not thereby cut off from society, disloyal to its due authority or unconcerned with what society is concerned with. There must be and is a ceaseless dialectical tension between the state and a church which insists that it is not the state, that it cannot regulate life in the way the state can, is not less concerned than the state with the whole of life, but cannot show that concern simply as a government chaplain. It is always a dangerous relationship, ceaselessly altering, but it is the only one that the inherent dualism of Christianity should really allow us.

It is a relationship which can hardly be maintained unless the church both truly believes in the Kingdom of God and is equally convinced that, however necessary the church may be, it is itself not the Kingdom (any more than the state is). Without a sense of the overwhelming primacy of a kingdom, of which it is quite genuinely no more than a servant and a signpost, the church is almost bound either to be so convinced of its own superiority that it can but strive to domesticate the state or to admit the claim of the state to ultimacy and allow itself to be domesticated by the state as its spiritual auxiliary. Two here and now ultimates are almost impossible to live with. It is the elusive reality of God's Kingdom, the embodiment of monism in the Ultimate but not before, which enables and requires dualism to endure in the penultimate, where the domestication of the state by the church is offensive to nature and the domestication of the church by the state offensive to grace. Both types of domestication are dangerous to everyone because by a premature merging of the two they either subject the pragmatic world of society and politics to an inappropriate religious control or, in allowing political control over the church, they naturalise it. Moreover, even within the natural order of the relationship of the political and the religious, they silence and prevent the possibility of a prophetic pointer to the transcendent challenging the existing structures, abuses and lies of secular power.

Our first model of the relationship of religion to society, once it grows beyond the stage of an unsophisticated absence of any perceived differentiation between the religious and the political, tends strongly either to an excessive sacralisation of the political order or an excessive secularisation of the church. In the Byzantine model the church 'blesses' the political institution, it unquestioningly applies Romans 13 to the benefit of almost any tyrant, while being expected to use whatever brain it may possess only in regard to the most recognisably religious of subjects: it may think about the Trinity, ikons, prayer, almsgiving, but not about the duties of government, the misdeeds of the security forces or the causality behind the predicament of the poor. Alternatively, the integration of church and state leads to an excessive ecclesiastical concern with secular matters of relatively secondary importance, perhaps superficially interpreted in over-ultimate and over-moral terms. This has been the case for much of Catholic history in the way that the church's concerns were determined by the immediate needs of the curia, the papal states, the ups and downs of Italian politics; it was the case for much early twentieth century British Nonconformity. The sectarian model, escaping from the world to pursue a wholly religious life, again rather easily moved from an excessively sacralised view of religion, of an over-dualistic kind, to an almost total preoccupation with the rearing of sheep or the running of a co-operative. One can see the social logic of this development working itself out in an often fascinating way in such examples as that of the Holy Apostles Community at Aiyetoro in Nigeria or, more slowly, in many a great Benedictine or Cistercian monastery.

Most Christian churches, nevertheless, do in fact in one way or another, according to their very different size, history, cultural relationship to the wider society and so forth, approximate most closely to our third model: an open relationship to the state which stops well short of integration. If a medieval type of society may make it hard to stop short, an inner thread of meaning in Christian tradition together with the structure of the ministry as it had developed from early times, are always there to speak up for dualism. There is something deeply repugnant to what one may call central Christian common sense in either a heavy erastianism, a theocracy or an unmitigated sectarianism. The church may put up with each for a time, even appearing to enjoy it, but it quickly either shrinks in vitality or finds paths to regain the middle way.

The contentious interface of church and state may, historically, be located in rather different areas, but the state in every age is concerned for a number of things in respect of religion and while in some circumstances it may judge an erastian mode the best way of obtaining them, in others the state will wish to eschew it. Religion must always matter to the state but unless society possesses a large measure of religious homogeneity, the erastian option can only land the state in quite unnecessary trouble. Erastianism or none, the state needs and wants a measure of uncontroversial but deeply felt 'civil religion'—religious sanctioning, blessing, support for the way it believes society should be; it fears to be challenged on any significant policy by an alternative authority internal to its society. Thus it is striking how the United States, constitutionally committed to the separation of church and state, yet plays incessantly upon the heart strings of civil religion. Every state seeks a broad cohesion between the political and the religious. What it fears as much as anything is a religiously-motivated intransigent minority determined to go its own way, dangerously out of step with public normality, thriving upon persecution. The heretic is flung to the lions, burnt, exiled, far more for socio-political than for genuinely religious reasons. But it seldom works.

The state rightly sees the church as always, potentially, a threat—that is why the possibility of controlling it through a benign establishment is so tempting. It recognises that religion is incurable but it also knows that a lion's teeth can often be brought to decay by a regular dose of sugar and that this is a very much more effective form of long-term control than flogging, racking and the rope. Finally, the more the state possesses its own ideological commitments, the more it is nationalistic, bellicose, socialist, monetarist or just protective of the interests of a particular class, the more it likes to see these particular causes appropriately furthered by the church. No state is without such, at least implicit, commitments. Again, there are bound to be painful casualties in war, there are bound in a capitalist-orientated society to be large discrepancies between the throw-away affluence of the rich and the pinching denial of the poor, there is bound in a socialist state to be no less a gap between the rhetoric and the reality of equality. In all these circumstances the state looks to the church not for criticism but for ideological support, for sermons and episcopal letters stressing that this is a just war in which God is only too pleased with some human sacrifice, that class differences between castle and cottage are divinely ordained, that Christianity and socialism are the same thing. The state in one way or another often wants a great deal from the church, and it often gets it.

The state is not wrong to want the support of religion, on the contrary; but one is not wrong either to exercise a vigorous suspicion in regard to every way in which it seeks that support— and one needs to exercise that suspicion for the health of the state no less than for that of the church, for only too often such support is achieved through a control which denies the church its proper freedom, and such a denial is as damaging to the state as it is to the church. Today when we say 'the church' we may well have in mind in this regard many other things too, particularly the universities, the BBC, the press. Between state and academe a dualism is no less needed for the health of both than between state and church. Our European universities were, indeed, in origin an extension of the intellectual life of the church and they carry today an important part of the church's traditional role. Just as in the later Middle Ages there was a creeping domestication of the church, so in our time is there a creeping domestication of the universities whereby the critical distance between university and government is more and more eroded. As this happens the churches, in the narrow sense, may actually recover aspects of their social role which they had largely forfeited to the universities and the media in a more genuinely liberal age. We have seen of late how this has been the case in eastern Europe where the churches remained the only considerable surviving institutions of an unstate-controlled mind. It could be so here too. In regard to every significant side of human life the church, whose primary concern is the preaching of the Kingdom, always retains a residual prophetic role, there to be reactivated when need arises. To be able to respond to that need it requires, even out of season, to look to its freedom.

The church, on its side, will also be looking for a range of benefits from a relationship with the state. Conflict with the state may arise from many different grounds, the church's first requirement being simply the freedom to exist. Conflict with the state has in many cases arisen from the latter's refusal to grant that freedom in a way consonant with the church's basic sense of identity. Early Roman persecutions, seventeenth-century Japanese ones, twentieth-century European ones all fit into this category. Church-state conflict is here a matter of sheer church survival, but such situations always presuppose the state's prior commitment to some other religion or ideology and its judgement that Christianity (or a specific church) is incompatible with that commitment. Here, for the Christian, the priority of dualism—the recognition of two authorities which may have simply to fight it out—is at its starkest and least avoidable.

A second type of church-state conflict is to be located within a large, not easily delimited, area where the church is struggling to retain essentially secular structures of power, influence, educational autonomy which the state sees as threatening to its authority, dangerous to society as a whole, or merely attractive to appropriate. Investiture, the functioning of church courts, monastic lands—to take a few medieval examples—or control of the missionary schools and hospitals set up in this century in Africa—to take a modern one, but the list could be extended almost indefinitely—represent matters all basically problematic. The church can hardly avoid ownership and it has a duty to serve society which may almost require the development of a great range of institutions. These things may give the church an apparently excessive degree of power (ownership of a third of the productive land in pre-Reformation England, it is estimated); their ecclesiastical control may become onerous to society and a genuine threat to the authority of the state to make reasonable decisions. The state may be justified in curtailing or confiscating them, though it may equally well be motivated by the greed of the powerful to the detriment of the real common good. In such conflicts the church has often been wrong yet it would be mistaken to say that the church should never fight over such things. It may even have a grave public duty to do so (as in South Africa in the 1950s when some churches struggled to keep their African schools despite the state's plans to take them over). An immense amount of church-state conflict falls within this area, an essentially messy area in which issues are seldom wholly clear and rights and wrongs can be argued over endlessly.

The principles behind their determination on the church side can be best elucidated if we pass on to a third area: the protection of the poor and oppressed, the cause of justice and truth against a tyrannical state—and few states are not at least slightly tyrannical. Thus Bishop Bell was prophesying to a state at war which claimed, not unreasonably, to be struggling for the cause of justice and truth itself, but was cutting too many corners in doing so. Here we are moving away from a concern with specific church institutions and activities to a far wider field mapped out by the condition of society more than the condition of the church. Yet they are still not unrelated. It is only through institutions of some sort, schools, youth movements, church-sponsored newspapers, cooperatives, or whatever, that the church can in any way struggle effectively with issues of justice and truth. It may well be that the church's concern in their regard has significantly shifted in this century. In the past its immediate concern was more for the institutions in themselves, seen as necessary for the sustenance of its own corporate membership and life; in the twentieth century the concern has been more clearly for what the institutions can actually achieve as instruments of service to society. The German Church struggle of the 1930s, subsequent struggles in Poland, South Africa and El Salvador, to take just a few examples, have grown increasingly disinterested. One underlying reason for this is, undoubtedly, a shift in ecclesiology linked with the growth of liberation theology. One keeps hearing people say they don't see how liberation theology is relevant to Britain or, more widely, the western world. I cannot agree. Liberation theology is in its essence simply a recognition that the core of all Christian life is concern for one's neighbour in need. If one serves the hungry, one serves the Lord, though wholly unaware that it is the Lord. If one does not serve the hungry, one does not serve the Lord, however often one cries 'Lord, Lord'. Such is the message of the judgement parable in Matthew 25 and the total logic of liberation theology is to be found herein. Secular liberation is the sacrament of spiritual liberation and only through the one can one enter into the other. Much traditional theology seemed to regard the former as almost peripheral to the Christian life and merely consequential to the latter. It may be that Latin American theologians of liberation have offered too narrow an analysis of secular liberation, but this is a secondary issue. The more such an understanding of the gospel becomes effectively central to the mind of the church, the more some forms of church-state conflict are likely to fade away but others come to the fore. A church committed to the primacy of an ecclesiology of liberation can hardly be a very erastian church because in every age and place government and those it is closest to tend to be either a very cause of oppression or at least unsympathetic to the underprivileged, the poor, despised minorities. A church proclaiming a gospel in terms of liberation theology has much greater need to be adequately distanced from government than a church proclaiming a rather other-worldly gospel, or, indeed, simply a this worldly message that commoners would be well advised to trust the great and the good. The problem with liberation theology is that, while not itself providing a social analysis, it rather calls for one to be made and if this is done simplistically, one-sidedly or in doctrinaire terms which purport to provide technical solutions to the world's problems of poverty and injustice but do not in fact do so, then the gospel itself may be discredited. Nevertheless a church's commitment to a liberation stance need not, and often should not, involve commitment to any specific analysis or programme for change. That is for individuals, action groups or political parties to work at and their specific conclusions—including the conclusions of some liberation theologians—are quite distinct from a theology or gospel of liberation itself.

If we accept that a dualist position fully open to the needs of society and enlightened by the underlying principle of the theology of liberation is that to which the church should now be committed in the public domain (and documents like *Faith in the City* and many others already suggest such a commitment), what should we think today of establishment, noting too the fact that Britain is much more pluralist in its religious belief and disbelief than it has been at any previous age in its history?

In the first thirty years of this century, the primacy of Randall Davidson, the real status of the Established Church in England underwent a profound alteration. The disestablishment of the Church in Wales, achieved finally in 1921, of four dioceses which hitherto had formed part of the province of Canterbury, showed close at hand what might be done. At the same time the Church Assembly, created by the church and empowered by Parliament through the Enabling Act, provided from 1919 a central, if not final, legislative authority for the Church in England of its own electing. Then in 1927 and 1928 Parliament rejected the revised Prayer Book approved by the Church Assembly in a large majority. The resultant impasse was discouraging for those who saw only too clearly that the church could no longer be plausibly controlled by a parliament as unAnglican as Westminster had now become and people spoke of disestablishment yet few really wanted it. The problem was shelved but it could not go away: someone had to govern the church and in practice this could now only be the church itself—the logic of the Enabling Act had to be extended rather than gone back upon—but a long inheritance of erastianism made this exceedingly uncongenial to most middle-of-the-road Anglicans. In consequence, during the second thirty years of this century, almost nothing was done, the world war being followed by the long neo-conservative primacy of Geoffrey Fisher, a natural erastian. It was the Indian summer of the established Church of England as of the British Empire. In the third thirty years, however, and especially in the primacy of Michael Ramsey, with his nonconformist roots, student Liberal politics and post-Tractarian ecclesiology, far more of a natural dualist, and during the heady reforming years of the 1960s, the legacy of 1928 was faced up to, and a revolution was brought about in the functioning of the Established Church. If one considers the establishment of General Synod, the Chadwick Report on *Church and State* of 1970 and the acceptance by Parliament of the substance of its proposals in regard to the regulation of worship and the appointment of bishops, 'revolution' is not too exaggerated a word. Even though the establishment of the church was not formally ended, the relationship of church and state did shift in these years from a basically monist to a basically dualist pattern. The revolution was hardly less for the fact that its agents were not quite aware of what they did.

Twenty years later it is time to ask: did these changes go far enough? Should the church at that moment of already major change, when faced with both the prospects of ecumenical unity with non-established churches (brighter then, alas, than they are now) and the new religious pluralism of Britain, not have gone the whole hog and opted for disestablishment? Three members of the Chadwick commission thought so and submitted a *memorandum of dissent*. There are certainly many Anglicans, and many non-Anglican Christians too, who agree with that minority and would regard the church and the majority of the Chadwick commission as hanging on to the now useless but still demeaning shreds of establishment for the sake of a watered-down mess of pottage garnished with sub-Hookerian fantasy.

What do we actually mean today by the 'establishment'? It is hard to answer with exactitude. In effect it covers two things: one, any legal status deriving from the Middle Ages, the sixteenth century or later, special to the Church of England as against other churches; two, a specific relationship with the state, laid down in essentials in the reign of Henry VIII and summarised in the two words 'Royal Supremacy'. The Chadwick Report does, I believe, fudge the latter. In practice 'establishment' means the coronation, the presence of bishops in the House of Lords, a rather limited measure of control by the Prime Minister over some church appointments, a good many rather erastian formularies. Personally I do not like the last two and they would still prevent me from becoming an Anglican, even if—for other reasons—I was tempted to do so, but in the life of the church they have now a fairly minor importance and I do not see why the Church of England can not move one or two steps further in line with the Scottish arrangement, whereby the Church of Scotland is established but is in no way controlled by parliament or crown. That would seem to me very desirable and I find some of the rather erastian argument in the Chadwick Report for not going that far unconvincing. Yet I do not think that this need lead to the ending of a special relationship with the crown, the ceremony of coronation or even the presence of bishops in the House of Lords, all of which I would prefer to see retained. These things do not, after all, depend upon the Royal Supremacy as declared by Henry VIII. They are, on the contrary, part of the inheritance of the medieval church which was basically dualist, not monist. Our coins declare Elizabeth *Regina Dei Gratia, Fidei Defensor.* None of that strictly depends upon the Henrician establishment and as the title 'Defender of the faith' was a papal award it should perhaps not be turned down in an ecumenical age! Why should the Church of England not quietly remove the last constitutional consequences of the Henrician revolution (it has, after all, already removed 90 per cent of them) while retaining the basic public status of establishment bequeathed to her by Magna Carta?

How, you may ask, can an anti-erastian like me finally come to carry the banner of antidisestablishmentarianism (to use what I have always been led to believe is the longest word in the English language)? How can I distrust the argumentation of the Chadwick Report and sympathise more with the sentiments of its minority *memorandum of dissent*, yet, finally, agree with the main thrust of its conclusion? It is not, primarily, because explicitly to seek 'disestablishment' would be to turn one's back rather too emphatically upon a very large chunk of our national religious history. It is not only that disestablishment would involve an enormous and damaging amount of internally directed activity, much of it cantankerous; and it is not just that it might well lead psychologically and socially to a considerable shift among clergy and laity in a rather sectarian direction, away from concern with the whole of the *humanum* and towards the purely religious. It is not even that the one really positive consequence of the state establishment seems to have been a remarkable, mostly creative measure of theological and spiritual freedom which could easily be lost with privatisation—it is noticeable that no other province of the Anglican communion has nourished nearly so clear a measure of comprehensiveness. It is, most of all, that while the establishment in the past was in principle erastian, Henrician and Justinianic, it today actually functions—so far as I can judge—far more as the servant of a healthy dualism. The Church of England is, today, clearly enough distanced from the state. While a strong establishment is bound to be erastian, a weak establishment may well be the best basis for the maintenance of a constructive dualism. Certainly it continues to bring the church a little closer to the centres of power than if it were disestablished. It brings MPs into St Margaret's, Westminster, to sing together *Songs of Praise* and, one hopes, on other occasions too. It keeps the lines of communications open, but no longer in a subservient way. On the contrary, it simply makes the wielders of secular sovereignty a little more aware of the reality of a different sovereignty. Nothing can prevent the church from being in many ways rather marginal to today's England. Establishment—if we can still call it that—seems to me now little more than retaining a chair upon which to stand as one tries to shout from the edge of the crowd. It would be silly to throw it away.

And it would be more than silly. It would actually be a betrayal of dualism in the name of dualism: a misreading of today's situation in response to belated remorse for yesterday's. Serious dualism involves the determination to be distinct from the state and yet potently concerned with what the state is concerned with: a hard enough task for any church, but a weak establishment may still make it just a little easier. Indeed it challenges the secularist monism which is in great danger of dominating our world far too powerfully. It is for this reason that I believe many religious non-christians—Hindus, Muslims, Sikhs and Jews— as well as many non-Anglican Christians like myself actually prefer some establishment to remain as a public symbol of the importance of religion, of belief in God, of the limits of Caesar's sovereignty. No age has needed such a symbol more. The more privatised the churches become, the less they can provide it. The establishment in its origin signified the victory of monism over dualism yet disestablishment would mean, I fear, simply another monist victory—bad for religion and bad for society because dualism is not merely a deep requirement of Christianity. It is also a requirement for a healthy society that the sovereignty of the state is never publicly unchallenged by the assertion of higher values.

The relations of church and state in this country are normally discussed in an almost purely English, and indeed Anglican, context. I was almost willing to try and do the same myself, but the more I entered into the subject, the more I found it would not work. English church-state relations have almost always included a third party—Rome and Catholicism—at the very least in the shape of Banquo's ghost at the banquet. The Anglo-Saxon origins of the relationship, its form in the thirteenth century, the sixteenth, the nineteenth, have always turned out to be triadic. In the 1920s Hensley Henson, an acute observer of his times, could still declare that 'the continuing conflict' with Rome remained 'the governing ecclesiastical issue' facing England. I find this to be true and to be the justification for the rather considerable amount of space I have devoted to it, as to the dualist tradition which from the time of Thomas More has been a signal contribution of English Catholics to the relationship of church and state, as it has been of most English Free Church Protestants. *Ecclesia Anglicana* in the thirteenth century, I have argued, was the public church of this land, but its underlying approach to the state remained essentially dualist in line with the central tradition of

Christian theology. At the Reformation the Church of England retained the public face but lost the dualism while the two minorities—Catholic and Free Church Protestant—lost the publicity but held on to the dualism. All three have since been integral parts of the English Christian tradition and all have something to contribute to the church-state relationship of the future, which, if it is to remain a living relationship, must be as ecumenical as the Christian consciousness and the life of the churches themselves has been becoming. A re-establishment of full communion between Canterbury and Rome seems highly unlikely in the foreseeable future, yet they have recognised each other as 'sister churches' and I don't believe the Church of England can now, any more than it could in the past, wisely disregard this relationship in shaping its other relationship with the state. The more the churches of this country, led by the Archbishops of Canterbury and Westminster, can function publicly as a sort of pragmatic unity, a sort of double-, triple- or quadruple-headed *Ecclesia Anglicana* (for the presence of the United Reformed Church and other representatives of the nonconformist tradition is no less to be included) the more we may claim that there still is in this country a publicly significant Christian church, a part of the *Catholica* which the Great Charter solemnly declared in the first of its clauses was to be free.

In our pursuit of a theme within the history of church and state, we have detected an almost endless oscillation between monism and dualism. Religion in general has both the social role of confirming and moralising the existing order and that of challenging and relativising it. The ebb and flow between confirming and challenging, between monism and dualism, is the very life of the political history of religion. Dualism represents the original Christian form of the relationship, almost inevitable—one may say—when the church was but a tiny minority yet I have suggested that there was more to it than that. Despite the rather monist model offered by the history of Israel and its kings, Christianity intrinsically requires a fair measure of distance between church and state if the message of the one who died *sub Pontio Pilato* is not to be seriously misrepresented. Nevertheless, once the church became a majority in society, the monist pull was inevitable and we have seen at least four forms of it—the Byzantine, the early western feudal, the high papalist and the post-Reformation erastian. While not too disastrous in the short run, where there is a conscientious ruler and no great theoretical pretensions behind his actions, monism soon jars with Christianity and produces a counter-resurgence of dualism, both theoretical and practical—Augustinian, papal, or Calvinist. In fact Christianity is inherently anti-monist and in consequence monist systems never really work very effectively. Even their most sincere proponents, like Cranmer or Sancroft, can be let down by them.

Today much of this may seem remote enough. There is not much danger of a Christian monism. The danger is rather the opposite—to move towards a sectarian dualism in which a minority church, over-preoccupied with its formulations of faith, its healing services, or whatever, is largely closed off from and unconcerned with political and secular society. The Christian commitment to dualism is one of immediate structure not of ultimate concern. Nothing is outside creation or the Kingdom of God. Immediate dualisms are encircled by an ultimate monism. Nature and grace are not, Aquinas tells us, to be confounded: *Gratia non tollit naturam sed perficit*—grace does not annihilate the natural but perfects it. In Augustine Christian dualism took a somewhat conflictual form. In Thomas the dualism remains but more harmoniously. The Thomist relationship of nature and grace found room for the thirteenth-century church's rather monist ideal but retains a sufficiently dualist structure to be serviceable in very different circumstances. The forms of dualism, of the relationship of church and state, are almost infinitely fluid and variable. What throughout them all is to be retained is a recognition of difference, the maintenance of a critical distance, but not the separation of two closed systems. At its best that is the lesson of both medieval and post-Reformation English experience. It is a lesson we can still afford to hear.

Epilogue

Establishment in the 1990s

In 1977, when still Bishop of St Albans, Robert Runcie gave a lecture entitled 'The Future of the Diocese' in the course of which he remarked, a propos of 'the shape of this institution in the future',

> I hope that St Albans Diocese will be part of a disestablished Church ... What is a National Church? A Church to which most of the nation belong? On any definition of belonging which would make it possible not to belong, most people do not belong to the Church of England. Yet if by a National Church is meant a Church which is concerned for the whole life of the nation and is sensitive to members who are seekers, then I observe my Roman Catholic, United Reformed Church and Methodist friends show no less openness ... I think that the Church will be disestablished, as Bishop Furse longed that it should be, and that my successors will no longer sit as of right in the House of Lords.
>
> (Robert Runcie (ed) *Cathedral and City*, St Albans Ancient and Modern 1977, pp. 129-30.)

I have the impression that Runcie as Archbishop of Canterbury changed his mind over this, probably because he had changed the viewpoint from which he considered it. When in 1985 there was some tension in the church because the House of Commons voted down a Synod measure about the appointment of bishops—a matter almost purely concerning formalities—he advised General Synod to play it cool: 'Much heat has been generated which threatens a partnership between Church and State in which the Church has been gradually achieving the ability to order its own affairs without seeking to break off the partnership.'

Today a diocesan bishop has for most of his purposes relatively little to do with the establishment, and in so far as he does encounter it he may—rather depending on his temperament—easily find it irksome. He has, of course, on appointment still to kneel before the Queen on a faldstool to do homage, his hands between hers, as he repeats the oath of allegiance. He is a member of the Board of Church Commissioners (although not necessarily a very active one) which administers a great deal of property for the good of the church, principally for the payment of clergy stipends, a Board which is finally responsible to Parliament as well as to the General Synod—though he may feel so out of sympathy with the policies of the Board that he will even take it to court, as the Bishop of Oxford has done. He will, sooner or later, be a member of the House of Lords. He will, more informally, be a member of a local establishment (considerably more so than the local Roman Catholic bishop, unless the latter achieves it by force of personality) civic, industrial, academic, and he will be able in consequence to exercise a little informal influence in many spheres of activity. Yet these all add up to a rather small part of the average bishop's work and many bishops actually resent the time they are still expected to give to being in London to take part in a Lords debate, even if they may also feel a little guilty at not giving the Lords more attention than they do. Below the level of a bishop, the 'establishment' of the church means even less. For many a vicar and practising church member it might be hard to say what impact it has at all on their lives to differentiate them from the lives of members of non-established churches, Roman Catholic, Methodist or Baptist. For non-church members it may, curiously, still mean a little more—the 'Church of England' remains vestigially special among churches with its ancient cathedrals, its prominent village and small town churches, its public panoply revealed in the wedding of a prince or the coronation of the sovereign. It may also still impinge at the point of marriage with the common law right to be married in the parish church, though it is a right which a steadily diminishing proportion of the population wishes to exercise.

   For an Archbishop of Canterbury, however, it is different. He at least still experiences the 'establishment' as a constant reality in his life. He is expected personally to minister to the royal family on special occasions; he knows that he may be called upon to crown the sovereign, his greatest public function; he attends frequent state banquets and other royal occasions as the Queen's first subject, taking precedence even over the Lord Chancellor and the Prime Minister. Again he is expected to speak in the House of Lords on major national issues—as bishops are not—and he may well be called to speak on them very publicly elsewhere too. His is a voice which, at moments of national importance, is expected to be heard. He is also in frequent touch with the Prime Minister over ecclesiastical appointments. A considerable amount of his time is thus spent administering to this 'partnership between church and state'. In the eight years between 1977 and 1985 Runcie had undoubtedly seen it at work in a way nobody else is able to do. He had revised his opinion. That revision is to be borne in mind.

If the Archbishop of Canterbury is the pivot of the relationship, then the appointment of a new archbishop is a good point at which to examine its functioning. This has just happened. Since 1977 there has been a formal procedure for such appointments which previously did not exist. A Crown Appointments Commission was established, chaired for the selection of bishops by one of the archbishops, for the selection of an archbishop by a lay person nominated by the Prime Minister. The Commission proposes two names to the Prime Minister in order, intimating that it prefers the first name but is happy also with the second. If the Prime Minister is unhappy with either, he may refer the case back to the Commission. In general these procedures appear to have worked hitherto to the satisfaction of both sides. The Prime Minister has not always accepted the first name but—at least in the case of any ordinary diocese—that would hardly seem calamitous. Effectively the church is now choosing its own bishops as it was not before 1977.

In the case of an archbishop, things are a little different. The Prime Minister's selection of a lay chairman already shapes the procedure in a slightly other way and may, conceivably, alter the balance of viewpoint within the Commission. The first chairman, in 1979 when Robert Runcie was recommended for Canterbury, was Sir Richard O'Brien, appointed by James Callaghan before the General Election of that year, although the nomination of Runcie was made by Margaret Thatcher a little after the election. In 1984 John Habgood was chosen for York by a Commission chaired by Dame Betty Ridley and in 1990 George Carey was chosen for Canterbury in a Commission chaired by Lord Caldecote. The three chairmen selected by the Prime Minister have all been people of distinction and outstanding experience, strong church members and good chairmen. Their selection could hardly be criticised on personal grounds. Moreover, while this procedure inevitably places a good deal of authority and some power in the hands of a person chosen by the state and possibly representative of a minority church view (but which church view is not a minority one?), it must be remembered that he or she is chairing a commission the core of whose membership is permanent and very experienced—far more experienced in this matter than the chairman. The chairman's power to affect the result should not be over-stated.

Normally the Archbishop of York should be a member of the

Commission to choose the Archbishop of Canterbury and the Archbishop of Canterbury will be a member of the Commission to choose the Archbishop of York. This provides the most senior possible voice of ecclesiastical authority within the Commission. If however—as in 1990—the Archbishop of York is a possible candidate for appointment to Canterbury, then of course he must forgo his place. It is certainly a pity to have no Archbishop on the Commission but the two bishops who were there in 1990 were both senior, John Baker of Salisbury and Ronald Bowlby of Southwark. With them were three clerical and three lay members nominated on a standing basis by General Synod and four *ad hoc* members from the vacancy-in-see committee of the diocese of Canterbury. The Secretary-General of the Anglican Consultative Council, Canon Sam Van Culin, an American, was present as a non-voting member, as were the Archbishops' Appointments Secretary and the Prime Minister's Appointments Secretary. It is clear that such a Commission can be said to represent the church and its range of interests responsibly, though it may be that in the special case of Canterbury it is over-weighted locally. It is a pity that the suggestion of the last Lambeth Conference that other primates within the Anglican Communion might be represented was not taken up. The choice of George Carey, of Bath and Wells, who had been a bishop for not much more than two years, was one accepted unusually quickly by Mrs Thatcher for nomination to the Queen.

There was here, undoubtedly, no ground for complaint upon either side within the context of the present arrangement, and it may seem to the observer an altogether admirable process. But there could have been. The choice of chairman could be controversial and did in fact raise just a little controversy this time on the grounds that Lord Caldecote had identified himself too closely with the most distinctively Protestant wing of the Church of England. Secondly, while it may matter relatively little in regard, say, to the diocese of Blackburn or Birmingham if the Prime Minister takes the second name and not the first, the same cannot be said in the case of Canterbury. It seems clear that in the three cases of archiepiscopal election the Prime Minister has always taken the first name but if he were not to do so, many people would very reasonably regard it as quite unacceptable. The exercise of a veto by the government in regard to the head of the church could, in the church's current state of mind, easily precipitate a crisis. Thus David Sheppard, the Bishop of Liverpool, was regarded as a highly likely candidate for Canterbury but many people wondered whether Mrs Thatcher might not refuse to nominate him on account of his outspoken opinions on social issues. Others wondered the same about John Habgood on account of his reputation for 'liberalism', a quality Mrs Thatcher was felt not to appreciate in bishops. Maybe these fears were in both cases groundless but it seems in principle deeply unsatisfactory that this could happen or even that the fear that it might happen could influence the deliberations of the Commission. If it did happen there would be a strong case for going further along the road to disestablishment. It would, anyway, be desirable that a convention should develop whereby it was agreed that in the case of an Archbishop the Prime Minister, having appointed the Commission's chairman, should then always agree to the first name.

The hope of many, and probably of Archbishop Runcie among them, is that the church can increase its freedom rather further without the cost, conflict and sheer loss of time involved in legal disestablishment. It is hard to see constitutionally why this should not be the case, so that the autonomy of an established Church of England *vis à vis* the state becomes no less than that of the established Church of Scotland.

Few people, who are both well informed about the actual working of the existing relationship and not in principle opposed to it, could really be enthusiastic for change, when they consider the immense amount of work which would be involved at many levels if legal disestablishment were to take place. Neither Parliament nor the church has the time to give to it. Nevertheless there are probably few churchmen today—certainly rather few members of General Synod—who are happy at the degree of residual control the state still exercises over the church. Equally there are a great many non-religious people who resent to some degree the apparently privileged state that the Church of England still enjoys. It is noticeable that they often mask their own resentment by using the argument that the establishment involves discrimination against other religious groups, Christian churches and non-Christian religions. Yet the latter themselves seldom these days appear to resent it, or indeed have much reason to do so. On the contrary they seem increasingly to regard the Church of England, and its spokesmen in the House of Lords, as convenient representatives of religion in general. It is also not true that Roman Catholic bishops, for instance, would like to share the episcopal seats in the Lords but they are content that Anglican bishops remain there. All are happy that individual religious leaders of distinction such as Donald Soper or George Macleod or the Chief Rabbi should be made life peers, but that is quite different from wanting any other institutional pattern of religious representation. In practice the Archbishop of Canterbury can increasingly be counted upon to speak up for the interests of Muslims or Jews when that is needed.

The Liberal Democrat Party voted overwhelmingly at its September 1990 annual conference for the disestablishment of the church although it seems unlikely that this motion will form part of its manifesto. The fact is that in today's very secular society both the Church of England and the concept of an established church are extremely remote from, and almost incomprehensible to, a very great many people, especially young people. It would be interesting to hold a Gallup poll on how many people could give intelligible answers to such basic questions as the special significance of the town of Canterbury or who the Archbishop of Canterbury is or what he is. The results might be surprising. The best case for disestablishment may well be the rather boring one that the gap is simply now too great between the country's common consciousness and the Church of England. Yet the gap may not be all that much greater, perhaps indeed considerably less, than in regard to the Lord Chancellor, the Warden of the Cinque Ports or, even, the General Secretary of the TUC. It would seem better for the health of society to go on carrying all sorts of minority-orientated structures and symbols within the country's total 'establishment', even some sheer bric-à-brac acquired from history, than to take the knife to anything which seems in part unadapted to a fairly simple conception of contemporary consciousness. A multicultural, pluralistic society may, conceivably, be seriously damaged by the continued entrenchment in power of Oxbridge graduates or achievers in the City; it can hardly be thought to be damaged by the continued status of the Archbishop of Canterbury. The central ritual tradition of the nation, relating particularly to the monarchy—and it is a tradition which is not a mere matter of ritual but of public morality too, a supra-party, socio-moral symbolism—would be enormously damaged by a total severing of the partnership. The monarchy would certainly lose far more of its deeper symbolic character than advocates of disestablishment usually recognise.

If the no-nonsense seculariser argues for disestablishment from one side, some church people do so out of almost greater conviction from another. For them the nature of the church is continually sullied by dependence of any sort upon Parliament. Its voice is rendered less credible, its motives impugned, its whole being is misread as but a historic symbolisation of national consciousness. When the erastian system was really strong, people were frequently too blind to its darker side or, when not blind, they left the state church for either nonconformity or Rome. When it is weak yet still just functioning, something one's conscience can cry out against on principle but no longer dangerously, then Constantine and his legacy may be the more fiercely denounced.

Certainly to anyone who has never been a member of a state church or in the context of the gospels and the early church, or again in the general context of world Christianity today, an established church is an anomaly. Even its defenders must recognise it as such. Yet the history of the church has been full of anomalies. Indeed it might be hard to imagine what a truly non-anomalous church would look like in the twentieth century. Anomaly, a great deal of it, has to be lived with by all of us. In the past, even up to the Second World War, the episcopal palaces, the stately vicarages, the clerical stress on being a gentleman, the enduring Barchester atmosphere of a good deal of the Church of England, was all profoundly alienating for large sections of common English humanity. Almost none of this exists today. It is hard to think that many people are seriously turned away by the surviving relics of privilege. The relationship remains odd, but then the construction of every socio-cultural tradition is odd to an outsider or even to a perceptive insider. The Christian church cannot exist without being local, and being local means adopting the odd particular flavour of a people's history.

It is hard to think convincingly of ways in which at present the Church's mission is significantly impeded by its establishment, very easy to think of ways in which it is significantly assisted. The whole exercise of *Faith in the City* and its follow-up, perhaps the most lastingly important thing that happened within the Church of England in the 1980s, could never have been mounted with the authority and scale that it had, without the sense that this was truly an exercise of the national church able to call on the resources of many outside the narrower frontiers of church membership.

If establishment is to be retained it will indeed be as a matter of provisionality. There is no final agreement in these things, particularly within a still divided Christendom. The Church of England does not find it hard to relate to the Church of France, whose primate, Cardinal Decourtray, has recently been making an official visit to Canterbury. One is established, the other is not. It makes relatively little difference either way. Archbishop Runcie has frequently stressed the inherent provisionality involved in the very existence of an autonomous Church of England at all or of an Anglican Communion not in communion with the Roman Catholic Communion and all else. The Church of England in its singularity is not part of the divine order. It is a provisional arrangement continued for want of a better. There is and always has been a deep ambiguity surrounding the very title 'Church of England'. How far is it, how far is it not, the *Ecclesia Anglicana* in full communion with the Pope and subject to his authority, which was referred to in 1215 by the Great Charter? How far are Robert Runcie and George Carey true successors of Augustine of Canterbury and of William Warham, the last pre-Reformation Archbishop? Enoch Powell, contributing to a set of essays entitled *The Synod of Westminster* (edited by Peter Moore, Dean of St Albans, 1986), defined the Church of England as follows: 'The Church of England is that Church of which the Supreme Governor on earth is the Crown of England.' For him this provides 'its essential characteristic, without which it would be something different in kind'. If that is true, then, essentially, it did not exist before 1533. It is essentially erastian and essentially different from every other part of the Anglican Communion. Is it conceivable that Henry VIII and Thomas Cranmer thought that they were creating something which did not until then exist? Could any Christian wish to belong to such a church and still be a Christian? Certainly in civil law and political and ecclesiastical order there was a new start in the sixteenth century, which should not be understated, coinciding with a process of liturgical reform and theological change of near revolutionary proportions. Yet Enoch Powell really goes the whole way with traditional Roman Catholic apologetic in so asserting the fundamentality of the Reformation settlement as to undermine the Church of England's Christian and historic credentials. Archbishop Runcie remarked in one of his last sermons in Canterbury Cathedral, in September 1990, honouring the seventh-century Archbishop Theodore, 'Let no one be fooled into thinking that the Church of England is a creation of the State.' Very few people today would wish to go along with Enoch Powell in defending the establishment on the ground that it is the essential characteristic of the Church of England. Most Christians would, on the contrary, think that if it were true then they could not possibly be, or remain, Anglicans. It is only in terms of seeing the significance of the establishment in very secondary terms that the state link remains tolerable. Nevertheless, it should not be doubted that Powell stands in such assertions, extravagant as they seem today, pretty close to a great deal of traditional broad church lay sentiment across the centuries.

He is encouraged and, to some small extent, even justified in his defence of the ecclesiastical supremacy of parliament by a certain unrepresentativeness in General Synod. When General Synod was established twenty years ago a great deal of effort was made to get its shape right, yet it seems not to have been entirely successful. Perhaps there is really no way in which the laity of a church, in all their degrees of commitment, can be at all adequately represented other than, symbolically and even pastorally, by vicar and bishop. The attempt to represent the laity by representative laity may be inherently mistaken in an episcopal church or, even, in any church. Yet the lay voice obviously needs to be heard in a range of forms and General Synod may offer too narrow a range at present. In Parliament it was heard in a different and still more narrow range—though it is entirely fallacious to read back into the takeover of the church by a royal and parliamentary coup in the sixteenth century a theology of lay authority. There was, perhaps, in it a pretty thin theology of royal authority, but of the authority of the laity next to none. Nevertheless it encouraged in due course a sense of lay responsibility, particularly as the balance of power between king and Commons altered. The Anglican tradition of lay responsibility in ecclesiastical matters, despite its abuse at times, needs to be healthily maintained and it is arguable that it could be better done than at present, though it is also rather easy to lambast the able and devoted people who give so much time to Synod matters: at present a popular game but not necessarily a very profitable one. What is quite certain is that General Synod represents the church as an active, committed, thoughtful body vastly much better than does Parliament.

If Mrs Thatcher continued to show a real interest in the church but never over-stepped current conventions as to the acceptable use of the Prime Minister's powers, Parliament has also not seriously threatened the viability of the present balance. Debates in the House of Lords, in particular, on ecclesiastical matters such as that of 3 July 1989 on the Clergy (Ordination) Measure remain examples of serious and valuable discussion from the reading of which anyone can profit. Enoch Powell's rather heavy sense of parliamentary supremacy over the church is not widely shared and is too idiosyncratic to matter very much. Nevertheless, present arrangements are capable of precipitating a crisis which few would desire on either side. The standing orders of Parliament's joint Ecclesiastical Committee (consisting of fifteen members from each House) were laid down in 1919 after the passing of the Enabling Act which established the Church Assembly. They were not revised, fifty years later, after the establishment of General Synod, as they should have been. In consequence, its members (who have mostly a great personal interest in religion but cannot conceivably be held representative either of church or nation in regard to religion) tend to ignore the implications of the partial disestablishment which did take place with the approval of parliament in the 1960s and 1970s and so to misjudge their present role. By interfering in ways no longer appropriate, they are in some danger of precipitating a church-state conflict quite unnecessarily.

The establishment of the Church of England remains, then, in contemporary terms somewhat anomalous—both in regard to English society and in regard to the Christian church elsewhere. But as both English society and the world church are full of anomalies, it is not to be rejected on account of that. It remains adequately but not overwhelmingly defensible on grounds of doing quite a lot of good and very little harm, of being part of a wider symbolic culture of the nation which we would be fools to dismantle, and of requiring for its termination a quite excessive amount of time and energy. If there were to be a strong attack upon it from other quarters of society, it could hardly be sustained—certainly not at the cost of prolonged controversy. Yet it is hard to see at present what significant part of society would really wish to mount such an attack: not other Christian leaders, not Jews, Muslims, Sikhs or Hindus, probably not the Labour Party.

A campaign of attack might conceivably be attractive to some of the tabloids and to some areas of white society looking for a 'radical' proposal to back which would not affect them one jot. Yet it seems doubtful whether even now there are any very large constituencies within the country so impervious to the church's role that such a campaign would be genuinely attractive. The church has a way of finding roads back into the inner city, suburbia, the countryside, even the upper classes. Only the Church of England itself, one concludes, might seriously set about the business of disestablishment, over-irritated by some rebuttal from Prime Minister or Parliament. It would be a pity were that to happen. Better to bite its lip and go on quietly seeking a Scottish solution. Keep the coronation, keep the bishops in the House of Lords, keep the Church Commissioners and as much as can be of the semi-formal links at lower levels, but cut away the surviving elements of parliamentary control over church order and Prime Ministerial control over the election of bishops—while recognising even there that for the time being it is being done responsibly. Maintain in fact as full as may be a public role for religion, and by no means an exclusively Anglican one (leaders of other churches have increasingly been brought into the great national ceremonies), while removing the traces of erastianism. Let *Ecclesia Anglicana* be free. The Great Charter was more fundamental to English history and freedom than the Reformation Parliament. Magna Carta and the Gospel seem a better guide than Constantine and Henry VIII for the future shape of the Church in England.

Further Reading

For New Testament origins, Oscar Cullmann's *The State in the New Testament* (SCM, London, 1955) remains useful. To it may be added *Jesus and the Politics of His Day*, eds Ernst Bammel and G. F. D. Moule (CUP, Cambridge, 1984), David Catchpole, *The Trial of Jesus* (Brill, Leiden, 1971) and Martin Hengel, *The Zealots* (T & T Clark, Edinburgh, 1989).

For the theory, one can still usefully begin with John Neville Figgis, *Churches in the Modern State* (Longmans, London, 1913) and Ernst Troeltsch, *The Social Teaching of the Christian Churches*, 2 vols (Allen and Unwin, London, 1931). The *Cambridge History of Medieval Political Thought, c.350–c.1450*, ed. J. H. Burns (CUP, Cambridge, 1988) is indispensable and highly authoritative. See also Walter Ullmann's *Principles of Government and Politics in the Middle Ages* (Methuen, London, 1961) a major study of both papacy and kingship by one of the greatest authorities, while A. P. D'Entreves' perceptive essay, *The Medieval Contribution to Political Thought* (Oxford, 1939), retains its value, especially for Hooker.

W. H. C. Frend, *The Rise of Christianity* (Darton, Longman and Todd, London, 1984) presents a masterly and massive survey of the first six centuries of Christianity. For Constantine the classical study is still N. H. Baynes, *Constantine the Great and the Christian Church* (1929, 2nd edition, Oxford, 1972) to which should be added T. D. Barnes, *Constantine and Eusebius* (Harvard University Press, 1981). The *Ecclesiastical History* of Eusebius is available in English in a two-volume edition with notes by H. J. Lawlor and J. E. Oulton (SPCK, 1928). Alistair Kee *Constantine versus Christ* (SCM, 1982) provides a stimulating theological analysis of the significance of Constantine's revolution. For Augustine see R. A. Markus, *Saeculum: history and society in the theology of Saint Augustine* (Cambridge 1970). Robin Lane Fox, *Pagans and Christians* (Viking, London, 1986) is splendidly enlightening for the third and fourth centuries and Judith Herren, *The Formation of Christendom*, (Blackwell, Oxford, 1987) for the sixth to the ninth.

Colin Morris, *The Papal Monarchy* (Oxford, 1989) provides the most recent account of the working of the medieval papacy. To it must be added R. W. Southern's two superb studies, *The Making of the Middle*

Ages (Hutchinson, London, 1953) and *Western Society and the Church in the Middle Ages* (Penguin, 1970).

Frank Gavin, *Seven Centuries of the Problem of Church and State* (Princeton, 1938) and Peter Hinchliff, *The One-Sided Reciprocity* (Darton, Longman and Todd, London 1966) offer wide-ranging surveys of the subject from past to present, while Edward Carpenter, *Cantuar* (Mowbray, London, 1971 and 1988) surveys all the archbishops of Canterbury at length.

Bede's *History of the English Church and People* has been published in many English translations including an edition in the Penguin Classics (1955). The later Saxon church is well served by Frank Barlow, *The English Church 1000–1066* (Longmans, 1963) and the post-Conquest church by his successor volume, *The English Church 1066–1154* (Longmans, 1979) and M. Brett, *The English Church under Henry I* (OUP, 1975). A. J. Macdonald, *Lanfranc* (Oxford, 1926), F. M. Powicke, *Stephen Langton* (Oxford, 1928) and David Knowles, *Thomas Becket* (Cambridge, 1970) have not been superseded, but for the last see also Frank Barlow, *Thomas Becket* (Weidenfeld and Nicolson, London, 1986). F. M. Powicke, *King Henry III and the Lord Edward* (Oxford, 1947, I, 259-66) provides an enlightening commentary on the role of the Papacy in the thirteenth-century English church, for which see also A. L. Smith, *Church and State in the Middle Ages* (Oxford, 1913), Z. N. Brooke, *The English Church and the Papacy* (Cambridge, 1931), C. H. Lawrence, ed. *The English Church and the Papacy in the Middle Ages* (Burns and Oates, 1965) and C. R. Cheney, *From Becket to Langton* (Manchester University Press, 1965).

A. G. Dickens, *The English Reformation* (2nd edition, Batsford, London, 1989) provides the most up-to-date survey of its subject; see also Claire Cross, *Church and People 1450-1660* (Harvester Press, 1976) for a longer view, together with A. E. Pollard, *Henry VIII* (Longmans, 1902), the classical biography and J. J. Scarisbrick, *Henry VIII* (Eyre and Spottiswoode, 1968), the most recent. Richard Marius, *Thomas More* (Dent 1984), Jasper Ridley, *Thomas Cranmer* (Oxford, 1962) and H. R. Trevor Roper, *Archbishop Laud* (revised edition, 1962) are all major biographies of leading actors in the church-state story. Jean-Pierre Moreau, *Rome ou l'Angleterre? Les Reactions Politiques des Catholiques Anglais au moment du schisme (1529–1553)* (Presses Universitaires de France, 1984) provides an extremely valuable new analysis by a non-Englishman of the central issues. The definitive edition of Richard Hooker, *Of the Laws of Ecclesiastical Polity*, is the Folger Library edition (Harvard University Press), 3 vols, 1977–81.

For the end of the seventeenth century, see G. V. Bennett, *The Tory Crisis in Church and State, 1688–1730* (Oxford, 1975), for the eighteenth century Norman Sykes, *Church and State in England in the Eighteenth Century* (Cambridge, 1934), for the early nineteenth, Robert Hole, *Pulpits, Politics and Public Order in England, 1760–1832* (Cambridge, 1989) and Olive Brose, *Church and Parliament, the Reshaping of the Church of England, 1828–1860* (Stanford University Press, 1959). The two volumes of Owen Chadwick, *The Victorian Church* (Black, London, 1966 and 1970) are a mine of enlightenment for Anglicanism in the nineteenth century. The most authoritative recent assessment of the nineteenth century is to be found in G. I. T. Machin, *Politics and the churches in Great Britain 1832 to 1868* (Clarendon Press, Oxford, 1977) and *Politics and the churches in Great Britain 1869–1921* (Clarendon Press, Oxford, 1987). David Nicholls, *Church and State in Britain since 1820* (1967) is an useful collection of documents. Edward Norman, *Church and Society in England, 1770-1970* (Oxford, 1976) surveys the last two centuries of Anglican social thinking.

The evolving attitudes of Gladstone, the most interesting if enigmatic nineteenth-century wrestler with the relationship of church and state, are discussed in Alec Vidler, *The Orb and the Cross* (1945), Perry Butler, *Gladstone, Church, State and Tractarianism* (Oxford, 1982) and J. P. Parry, *Democracy and Religion, Gladstone and the Liberal Party, 1867–1875* (Cambridge, 1986) and revealed in the massive two volumes of *Correspondence on Church and Religion of William Ewart Gladstone*, ed. D. C. Lathbury (John Murray, 1910).

G. K. A. Bell's *Randall Davidson*, 2 vols (Oxford, 1935) is an exceptionally authoritative and detailed biography of the most important figure in modern Anglican church history. To it should be added a number of other 'official biographies': J. G. Lockhart, *Cosmo Gordon Lang* (1949), F. A, Iremonger, *William Temple* (Oxford 1948), R. Jasper, *George Bell* (1967) and Owen Chadwick, *Michael Ramsey* (Clarendon, Oxford, 1990). We still await the biography of Geoffrey Fisher. For Bell see also Kenneth Slack, *George Bell* and Peter Walker, *Rediscovering the Middle Way* (Mowbray, London, 1988), especially chapter 7, pp. 62-70.

D. W. Bebbington, *The Nonconformist Conscience, Chapel and Politics, 1870-1914* (George Allen and Unwin, London, 1982) is the best recent introduction to the greatest political age of Nonconformity, but see also Stephen Koss, *Nonconformity in British Politics* (1975).

Edward Norman, *Roman Catholicism in England*, (Oxford, 1986) is the best short history of the subject, and John Bossy, *The English Catholic Community 1570–1850* (Darton, Longman and Todd, London, 1976) the best longer one. Arnold Pritchard, *Catholic Loyalism in Elizabethan England* (University of North Carolina Press, 1979) examines the relationship of Catholicism to patriotism in the sixteenth century, while Edward Norman's *Anti-Catholicism in Victorian England* (George Allen and

Unwin, London, 1968) is valuable for the nineteenth. Two books on Manning are important: V. A. McClelland *Cardinal Manning, his public life and influence* (Oxford, 1962) and Robert Gray, *Cardinal Manning* (Weidenfeld and Nicolson, London, 1985). For the 1930s and 1940s see Thomas Moloney, *Westminster, Whitehall and the Vatican, The Role of Cardinal Hinsley 1935–43* (Burns and Oates, 1985) and Owen Chadwick, *Britain and the Vatican during the Second World War* (Cambridge, 1986).

For the present and future of the establishment see, especially, the Chadwick Report of 1970, *Church and State* (reprinted 1985, Church Information Office, London). The position of the established church after Parliament's rejection of the revised prayer book was considered by an earlier report entitled *Church and State*, published in 1935, produced by a Commission appointed by the Archbishops and chaired by Viscount Cecil of Chelwood. Cyril Garbett's *Church and State in England* (Hodder and Stoughton, 1950) is still worth consulting for the pre-Chadwick Report era. The case for a continued establishment today may be found in John Habgood, *Church and Nation in a Secular Age* (Darton, Longman and Todd, 1983), especially chapter 6, the case against in Peter Cornwell, *The Church and the Nation: the Case for Disestablishment* (1983) as also in Valerie Pitt's *Memorandum of Dissent* to the 1970 *Church and State* report (pp. 68-79). *The Church and the State*, ed. Donald Reeves (Hodder and Stoughton, 1984) presents a range of views, as does George Moyser, ed. *Church and Politics Today: The Role of the Church of England in Contemporary Politics* (T & T Clark, 1985). See also Gareth Bennett, *To the Church of England* (Churchman Publishing, 1988), chapter 4 'The Royal Supremacy: a theological assessment'.

K. N. Medhurst and G. H. Moyser, *The Church and Politics in a Secular Age* (Oxford 1988) provides a good introduction to current issues. Adrian Hastings, *A History of English Christianity 1920–1985* (Collins, London, 1986) includes a good deal about church-state relations in the twentieth century. Finally, for a general analysis of the whole range of possible church-state relations, see 'A typology of church-state relations' in A. Hastings, *The Faces of God* (Geoffrey Chapman, London, 1976 pp. 47-67).

Index

Aberdeen, 30
Acton, Lord, 46
Aiyetoro, Holy Apostles
  Community, Nigeria, 56
Alabama, Bishop of, 30
Alfred, King, 11, 19
Anastasius, Emperor, 9
Andrews, C.F., 38
Anglican Consultative Council, 70
Aquinas, Thomas, 17, 22, 66
Argyll and the Isles, Bishop of, 30
Arnold, Thomas, 27-8
Asquith, Herbert, 41
Athanasius, St, 7
Augustine of Canterbury, 10, 73
Augustine of Hippo, 7, 9, 18, 66
Augustus, Emperor, 7, 9
Avignon, 20

Baker, John, Bishop, 70
Balfour, Arthur, 41, 54
Barbados, Bishop of, 30
BBC, 31, 58
Becket, Thomas, Archbishop, 12-15
Bede, the Venerable, 10
Bedford Gaol, 23
Bell, George, Bishop, 51-3
Belloc, Hilaire, 45
Bombay, 37
Boniface VIII, Pope, 12
Bourne, Francis, Archbishop and
  Cardinal, 41, 44, 48
Bowlby, Ronald, Bishop, 70
Boyne, Battle of, 34
Bracton, Henry, judge, 20
Brandon, S.G.F., 1
Bray, Vicar of, 24

Bunyan, John 23
Butler, R.A., 45

Caldecote, Lord, 69-70
Canada, 30, 37
Canterbury, 9-15, 21, 23, 25, 29, 31-2,
  52, 65, 67-70, 72
Carey, George, Archbishop, 69-70, 73
Catholic Emancipation Act, 26, 38
Ceolwulf of Northumbria, King, 10
Chadwick, Owen, 26, 62
Chadwick Report on *Church and
  State*, 62-3
Chamberlain, Neville, 41
Charlemagne, 8, 17-18
Charles I, King, 24
Charles II, King, 23-4
Chief Rabbi, 71
Choblet, Father, 39
Church Assembly, 31, 61, 75,
Clifford, John, 54
Commons, House of, 35, 50, 63, 67,
  75
Constantine, Emperor, 5-8, 18, 22,
  25, 72, 76
Constantinople, 8, 21, 24, 42
Constantius, 7
Convocations of Canterbury and
  York, 25, 29, 31
Cranmer, Thomas, Archbishop, 21,
  66, 74
Crewe, Lord, 41
Cripps, Arthur Shearly, 38
Cromwell, Oliver, 23, 53
Cromwell, Thomas, 20
Crown Appointments Commission,
  69-70

Cyprian, 5
Cyprus, 2

Damasus, Pope, 9
Davidson, Randall, Archbishop, 31-2, 48, 51, 61
Decourtray, Cardinal, 73
Declaration of Indulgence, 23-4
De Salis, Count John, 42-3
Disestablishment, 30, 61, 63, 67, 71-2
Donation of Constantine, 18
Dunstan, Archbishop, 11, 14
Durham, Bishops of, 31

Ecclesiastical Titles Act, 1851, 49
Eden, Anthony, 41
Edict of Nantes, Revocation of, 35
Edmund of Abingdon, Archbishop, 14
Education Act, 1902, 49, 54
Edward VII, King, 41, 43
Elizabeth I, Queen, 30, 33-4
Elizabeth II, Queen, 30, 63
Establishment, 8, 14, 17-18, 20, 22-4, 27, 30-1, 52, 54, 57, 62- 4, 67-9, 71-6
Ethelbert of Kent, King, 10
Eucharistic Congress, 1908, 41
Eusebius of Caesarea, Bishop, 6-8

Faith in the City, 61, 73
Fisher, Geoffrey, Archbishop, 32, 52, 61
Fisher, John, Bishop and Cardinal, 21
FitzAlan-Howard, Edmund, 42-3
Foliot, Gilbert, Bishop, 13
Forsyth, P.T., 22
Free Churches, 23, 25-6, 53-4, 65

Gasquet, F.A., Cardinal, 43
Gelasius, Pope, 9, 12
General Strike, 31, 51
General Synod, 29, 31, 62, 67-8, 70-1, 74-5
Geneva, 20, 22
George V, King, 42-3

Gladstone, William, 27-30, 37, 46
Godfrey, William, Archbishop and Cardinal, 43
Gorham Judgement, 28
Gregory the Great, Pope, 9-10, 19
Gregory VII, Pope, 12, 19
Grimble, Arthur, 39
Grosseteste, Robert, Bishop, 20
Gunpowder Plot, 33-4

Habgood, John, Archbishop, 69
Hatfield, Synod of, 9
Henry II, King, 13, 15
Henry III, King, 14-15
Henry VIII, King, 15, 20, 22, 36, 62-3, 74, 76
Henry, Sir Edward, 41
Henson, Hensley, Bishop, 64
Hinsley, Arthur, Archbishop and Cardinal, 42, 44, 48-9
Hooker, Richard, 22-3, 28, 55
Hope, James, 42
Horne, Sylvester, 54
Howard, Sir Henry, 43
Hugh of Lincoln, Bishop, 17
Hume, Basil, Archbishop and Cardinal, 50

India, 37, 40
Innocent XI, Pope, 36
Internment of enemy aliens, 52
Ireland, 27, 29-30, 37-8, 40, 42
Isaiah, prophet, 2
Islam, 3-4, 18, 55

James II, King, 23-4, 32, 35-6
Jeremiah, prophet, 2
Jews, 1-2, 17, 28, 52, 71
John, King, 13
Julian, Emperor, 6
Justinian, Emperor, 8, 17-18, 21-2, 55

Keble, John, 27
Ken, Thomas, Bishop, 24
Kingdom of God, 1, 19, 55-6, 58

Index

Labour Party, 25, 76
Lambeth Conference, 30, 32, 70
Lambeth Palace, 25
Lanfranc, Archbishop, 11
Lang, Cosmo, Archbishop, 49
Langton, Stephen, Archbishop and Cardinal, 12-15, 19, 32
Lateran Council, IV, 14
Laud, William, Archbishop, 23
Leo I, Pope, 9
Leo XIII, Pope, 40-1, 43, 46, 48
Liberal Party, 25, 37, 53-5, 71-2
Liberation Theology, 60-1
Liberius, Pope, 7
Life and Work, 52
Lloyd George, David, 51, 54
London, 10, 12, 29, 41
Lords, House of, 31, 49-50, 54, 62-3, 68, 71, 75
Louis XIV, King, 35-6
Louisiana, 30
Lugard, F., 38-9

Macleod, George, 71
Magna Carta, 13-14, 63, 65, 73, 76,
Malta, 37-8
Manning, Henry, Archbishop and Cardinal, 27-32, 45-8
Mannix, Archbishop, 49
Marshall, Sir James, 39
Maryland, 26
Mathew, David, Archbishop, 50
Maynooth Grant, 38
Mengo, Battle of, 38
Merton, Council of, 20
Milan, Edict of, 6
Mill Hill Fathers, 39
More, Thomas, 21-2, 35-6, 43
Moscow, 24
Muhammad, 3-4, 7

Newman, John Henry, Cardinal, 27-8, 45-7
New Zealand, 30
Nicomedia, 5
Nonconformist conscience, 53-4

Non-Jurors, 24-5
Norfolk, 15th Duke of, 28, 39, 41-3, 46-7

Obliteration bombing, 52
O'Brien, Richard, 69
O'Connell, Daniel, 27
O'Conor, Nicholas, 42
Oratory School, Birmingham, 42, 47
Osborne, d'Arcy, 44

Papacy, 7, 9-14, 18-19, 34, 36, 39-41, 43-5, 48, 64
Parliament Act, 1910, 31
Patrick, Mother, 39
Patterson, Bishop, 39
Penn, William, 23
Pilate, Pontius, 1, 8
Pius V, Pope, 33, 36
Pius IX, Pope, 46
Pius XI, Pope, 44-5
Pius XII, Pope, 44
Pontigny, 12-13
Powell, Enoch, 73-5
Prayer Book Controversy, 1927-8, 61

Quakers, 23, 25, 28
Quebec, 37-8

Ramsey, Michael, 61
Reformation, the, 20-1, 65
Reith, J.C.W., 31
Rhodesia, 39
Ridley, Dame Betty, 69
Ripon, Marquis of, 37, 39, 41, 46
Roman Empire, 1-2, 4-9, 11, 17
Rome, Church of, 7, 11
Runcie, Robert, Archbishop, 67, 71, 73-4

Saint Bartholomew's Day, 34
Saint Edmund's House, Cambridge, 47
Salisbury, Earl of, 30-1, 42
Sancroft, William, Archbishop, 24, 66
Scotland, 22, 24, 30, 32, 62, 71

Seabury, Samuel, Bishop, 29
Sheppard, David, Bishop, 29
Sheppard, Dick, 52
Soper, Donald, 71
South Africa, 59-60
Syllabus of Errors, 46
Sylvester, Pope, 7

Tait, Alexander, Archbishop, 29, 31
Temple, William, Archbishop, 52-3
Tennessee, Bishop of, 30
Tertullian, 5
Thatcher, Margaret, 69-71, 75
Theobald, Archbishop, 13-14
Theocracy, 12, 16, 18, 22, 57
Theodore of Tarsus, 9-11, 14, 19, 32, 74
Toleration, 23, 25-6
Tory views, 23-4, 28
Tresham, Thomas, 35
Trinidad, 37

Uganda, 38-9
United States of America, 26, 29-30, 57

Van Culin, Sam, 70

Vaughan, Herbert, Archbishop and Cardinal, 42, 48
Victoria, Queen, 30-1, 43

Wales, 30, 61
Walpole, Henry, St, 35
Warham, William, Archbishop, 21, 73
Waugh, Evelyn, 35
Westcott, B.F., Bishop, 31
Westminster, Archdiocese of, 27, 29, 48, 65
Weston, William, S.J., 35
White Fathers, 38
Wilberforce, Samuel, Bishop, 29
William I, King, 11, 13
William III, King, 23, 33
Winnington-Ingram, Arthur, Bishop, 51
Wiseman, Nicholas, Archbishop and Cardinal, 27
Wolsey, Thomas, Archbishop and Cardinal, 20-1

York, 10, 21, 29-31, 38, 69-70

University of Exeter Press

Other titles include:

The Human Embryo
Aristotle and the Arabic and European traditions
edited by G.R. Dunstan

The Jewish Communities of South-West England
Their rise and decline, 1100 to the present
Bernard Susser

The Great East Window of Exeter Cathedral
A glazing history
Chris Brooks and David Evans

The Minor Clergy of Exeter Cathedral 1300-1548
Nicholas Orme

Exeter Studies in History
Human History and Social Process
Johan Goudsblom, E.L. Jones and Stephen Mennell

Unity and Variety
A History of the Church in Devon and Cornwall
edited by Nicholas Orme

Exeter Studies in American and Commonwealth Arts
Locating the Shakers
Cultural origins and legacies of an American religious movement
edited by Mick Gidley with Kate Bowles

For details of these and all titles published by the University of Exeter Press, please contact: The Sales Office, University of Exeter Press, Reed Hall, Streatham Drive, Exeter EX4 4QR, UK. Telephone: (0392) 263066 (1 pm to 5 pm or ansafone).

www.ingramcontent.com/pod-product-compliance
Ingram Content Group UK Ltd.
Pitfield, Milton Keynes, MK11 3LW, UK
UKHW042121200326
4879IPUK00001B/3